Steve Allen is an entertainer who occupies the very top echelon of his profession. Yet along with his ability to entertain, he possesses perhaps a more important distinction: the ability to think intelligently and feel deeply. Mr. Allen's humanitarian concern is at the core of his personality, and appropriately, it has made him, in addition to being one of America's most popular showmen, one of its most respected. Born in New York, Steve Allen now lives in Encino, California.

THE GROUND IS OUR TABLE

Books by Steve Allen

THE GROUND IS OUR TABLE

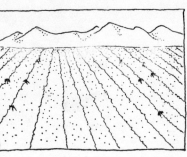

by *Steve Allen*

With photographs by Arthur Dubinsky

". . . we're tickled anyway when we work a little. We can feed our children. Half eat. The road became our home. The ground is our table."

—A CALIFORNIA FARM WORKER

DOUBLEDAY AND COMPANY, INC., GARDEN CITY, NEW YORK

Library of Congress Catalog Card Number 66–24316
Copyright © 1966 by Steve Allen
All Rights Reserved
Printed in the United States of America

Statement by Raul Aguilar is reprinted from *Report on Farm Labor*, 1959, by permission of the National Advisory Committee on Farm Labor.

Statement by John Zuckerman, a Stockton, California farmer, is reprinted by permission of Mr. Zuckerman.

CONTENTS

FOREWORD

At the moment you hold this book in your hand an American child is lying in a rural hovel, ill unto death. He has never gotten the kind of health-care he would have enjoyed in the city. His parents have no money saved to pay for visits by a doctor or treatment at a hospital.

It would be dramatic to say that you can help that child. The harsh reality is that you cannot. He will die.

His last feverish sight will be of a weeping mother, an embittered or perhaps totally defeated father, behind them frightened, confused brothers and sisters, and a blurred collage of a small room, unpainted walls, broken-down furniture, discolored windows, and a bare, drafty floor.

During his short pathetic life he will have played with few toys. Those few will have been secondhand.

If he has gone to school at all, his schooling will have been so inferior that he will have lagged two years behind city children of the same age.

No, you cannot help him. His fate has been sealed by powerful social forces the flow of which cannot be stopped in a moment.

But these forces are not irresistible. You can affect their

future course. It is my purpose to induce you to make the effort.

For countless centuries man has lived and struggled in a hard world. Even today two thirds of the human race live in poverty. But that such conditions should be common in 1966, in the wealthiest nation on earth, is morally intolerable because *it is no longer inevitable or necessary.*

I do not propose to deal, in this brief volume, with the total problem of poverty in the United States. My canvas is limited, but the picture it reveals is ugly. Fortunately you have the power to alter that picture. Accept the challenge and fewer rural children will live and die in squalor, fewer mothers will endure a life of endless drudgery, fewer fathers will be treated like second-class citizens.

Let us start with a question.

THE GROUND IS OUR TABLE

I WEIGHTED SCALES

I

Which weighs more: a tomato or a person? I urge you to take this question seriously, for the assumptions which lie behind your answer may help determine whether hundreds of thousands of America's farm workers will receive just or unjust treatment.

It seems gruesome, but many people have read the scale in favor of the tomato and because they have, life will be no different for the men, women, and children who harvest the bounty of our fields, orchards, and groves. They will continue to lead dreary lives of poverty, illiteracy, and malnutrition. If, however, you read the scale in favor of the human being, life may hold for the farm workers of America what it has never held before—a living wage for honest labor, an opportunity to build a home, a promise that the future will be brighter for their children than it has been for themselves.

Where does this choice confront you—this choice between justice or injustice, squalor or decency? It can confront you in your supermarket, in your newspaper headlines, in your everyday conversation, in your own heart.

What worries you most: the possibility of a slight rise in food prices or the hard reality of poverty-level wages for those who start the food on its journey to your tables? What angers you more: vague allusions to supposedly rotting crops or stark facts depicting rotten living conditions for the families of farm workers? What annoys you more: United States Senators wringing their hands in mock anguish or unemployed American citizens hanging their heads in genuine despair? Answer these questions and you will have read the scale, been confronted by a moral choice.

This book deals with the dilemma of the farm worker in the United States, chiefly in the Southwest. It is written, I concede, in anger. I do not apologize for the fact that it is partly a personal account. Nor do I pretend that the book is a literary achievement or a scholarly work by professional standards.

I am perhaps better qualified than some professional sociologists and farm labor experts, however, to discuss poverty and squalor for the reason that I have personally experienced both. While my family never suffered that long-term, spirit-grinding poverty that eventually stunts the minds and souls of practically all who endure it, there were, nevertheless, periods when we were reduced to living in hideously depressing quarters and subsisting on meager fare.

As I look back over that time of my early life, an endless succession of cheap, furnished rooms flashes across my mind. The cockroaches could never be driven from those kitchenettes, nor the bedbugs from the mattresses, nor the rats from the walls. But I was young and on the way up and out of such an environment. Thousands who lived around me were old, hopelessly defeated, and sentenced by fate or society to a seeming eternity of miserable existence.

I remember in particular an old woman with cancer of the face, who lived in the room next to us in a run-down apartment on Chicago's South Side. Her simple physical presence was frightening. I tried to shut my mind to her existence, as much as was possible. Sometimes I would see drops of blood on the carpet near her door, and if the door to her room was open, I would see her staggering aimlessly about, rubbing her face with bloody rags. She was completely alone in the world—whether single, widowed, or divorced I never knew. She rarely spoke to us nor we to her, but I have the faint recollection, after all these years, that she had a foreign accent, German, I think. It is uncomfortable even now to recall this forlorn woman, but my memory of her serves as a reminder of the loneliness and helplessness of life on the lowest levels of our affluent society, of the despair from which we willfully turn away.

Once you have experienced real poverty, or been intimately acquainted with it, you can never put its reality out of your mind—unless your soul is a dead and shriveled thing. It was Michael Harrington's experience with Dorothy Day's *Catholic Worker* group in New York City that led to his dedication in combating poverty and to the writing of his incisive book *The Other America*.

John Cogley, another one-time member of *The Catholic Worker* staff, has told me that the things he saw as a young man, working among the poor in New York, made such a powerful impression on him that often at the end of his day's work he would drive off somewhere in his car and just sit there awhile weeping, out of the feeling of sheer frustration at his inability to do any more than feebly struggle against the twin curses of poverty and squalor.

George Orwell, in *Down and Out in Paris and London*, has given perhaps as clear a picture of poverty as words can convey. "It is altogether curious, your first contact with poverty. You have thought so much about poverty . . . and it is utterly and prosaically different. You thought it would be quite simple; it is extraordinarily complicated. You thought it would be terrible; it is merely squalid and boring. It is the peculiar *lowness* of poverty that you discover first; the shifts that it puts you to, the complicated meanness, the crust-wiping. . . . Mean disasters happen and rob you of food. You have spent your last eighty centimes on half a liter of milk, and are boiling it over the spirit lamp. While it boils a bug runs down your forearm; you give the bug a flick with your nail, and it falls, plop! Straight into the milk. There is nothing for it but to throw the milk away and go foodless . . . one could multiply these disasters by the hundreds. They are part of the process of being hard up.

"You discover what it is like to be hungry . . . that a man who has gone even a week on bread and margarine is not a man any longer, only a belly with a few accessory organs . . . you also discover the great redeeming feature of poverty: the fact that it annihilates the future. . . . When you have only three francs you are quite indifferent; for three francs will feed you until tomorrow, and you cannot think further than that."

As powerfully descriptive as Orwell is, the printed word can never equal the impact of one's own physical confrontations with hunger and poverty. I can recall, on a California morning long ago, hitchhiking west to Los Angeles and being so hungry that when I saw a discarded pork-and-beans can I picked it up, discovered that it still held eight or ten beans, scooped them out with my bare and unclean fingers, and—blowing off a swarm of ants—wolfed them down.

I remember another time when, to speak plainly, hunger drove me to steal. I went into a grocery store in New Mexico with only enough change in my pocket to buy a loaf of bread. I paid for the bread but concealed a can of sardines in my pocket. Outside, I ducked around the corner, sat down on the sidewalk, opened the can with trembling hands, and stuffed myself with five or six sardine sandwiches. It is of enormous significance that hunger simply annihilated guilt.

I relate these personal experiences by way of arguing that hunger, poverty, and squalor rob man of the dignity that can so gloriously be his. Hunger defeats what is human in man. He must never be allowed to exist merely as a carnivorous animal, functioning only to find his next meal and convert it to waste.

It is only with a minimum of physical security that he can turn to those more edifying purposes which all religious philosophies tell us are his highest object. Certainly many poor people are religious, but the poorest of the poor often lose interest in the church—perhaps through despair. When the poor are *that* poor, they are often regarded as hopeless, too troublesome, an annoyance, and an affront to decency. Sad to say, this attitude is not foreign to some ordained representatives of our churches. The kind of poor who conveniently salve our consciences are those who simply need the loan of a few dollars, or a Christmas basket, or a couple of days' work, or the gift of some clothes we didn't want to wear again anyway.

II

I do not consider myself a foe of the farm industry but its friend. I have perhaps done more, in my sixteen years in television, to promote and publicize farm produce than anyone else in the industry.

Initially this came about by accident when we booked one of those attractive young bathing-suited ladies who are forever being selected Miss Grapefruit, Miss Artichoke, Miss Watermelon, or Miss Celery—obviously for promotional reasons. Ordinarily such models do nothing more than pose for pictures, but in the case of the young lady we engaged, a New York publicist had conceived the bright idea that it might be helpful if she was interviewed on the program. The interview turned out to be highly amusing, largely because the young lady was completely innocent of the intricacies of raising and marketing strawberries, cauliflower, or whatever it was she was promoting. From that moment, the appearance of such personable young publicists has been a regular feature of my television programs, with the result that I have been widely publicized in farm and food-industry journals as a friend of agriculture.

The friendship has grown in other ways. Because fruits and vegetables form an important part of the diet of the Allen family, my television desk has frequently been decorated with a basket of mixed fruit, and I have often sipped fruit juices in the public view. I am grateful to the various food-produce firms which have sponsored my television programs over the years, and I am aware that our nation must show painstaking concern for the economic health of the industry that provides us with food and nourishment. I endorse whatever programs—be they conceived by the state or by industry—that will sustain and encourage our growers. But I insist equally that the food industry is not morally justified in denying social justice to the hundreds of thousands of American citizens without whose toil the industry itself would collapse overnight.

I

I love the Southwest. Two of its great cities, Phoenix and Los Angeles, I can call home. I like the easygoing way of life, the many friendly people, the scenic beauty, and the sense of the romantic past that the area has managed to preserve. And because I feel so at home in the Southwest I am concerned about the squalor in which eight million of its citizens live.

Part of my concern is motivated by attachment to the Mexican-Americans who constitute the great majority of farm workers in the Southwest. I shall never forget the kindness shown me by these people years ago when I ran away from home in Chicago and bummed my way around the country before ending up in Los Angeles. When I ran out of money in Texas, I naturally resorted to the time-honored method of keeping body and soul together—begging for food or money or offering to do odd jobs in exchange. The socially proper whites whom I approached in Texas, New Mexico, Arizona, and California treated me, for the most part, abruptly, contemptuously, and uncharitably. But I never put the touch on a Mexican-American without his responding with a nickel, a *taco*, a *taco* with a few beans rolled up in it, *something*. The Spanish tradition, which influences the most ignorant and poverty-stricken Mexican-American in the same way that the English tradition influences the majority of Americans, is one in which true charity is fundamentally important.

The Southwest is an area of sharp and dramatic economic contrasts. Enormous wealth has been accumulated through oil, cattle, copper, grain, cotton, vegetables, fruit, and real estate. Against this backdrop of affluence, there are communities in which the average family income is less than $1500 per year. Thousands of people somehow eke out a living on an annual income of less than $800. In the five Southwestern states as a whole roughly *one fifth* of the population lives in dire poverty.

These and other equally shocking facts were brought to my attention in January, 1965, when I attended the President's Conference on Poverty in the Southwest. Delegates were addressed by Vice President Hubert Humphrey, Anti-Poverty Chief Sargent Shriver, Jackie Robinson, Father James Vizzard, S.J., of the National Catholic Rural Life Conference, and other distinguished citizens. Representatives of private and state agencies concerned with the poor sketched in graphic detail the monumental task before us.

The statistics revealed were alarming, the stories of personal tragedy and bravery were moving. Clearly the Southwest is faced with a situation that demands relief. Catholic Archbishop Robert Lucey of San Antonio, long a champion of the underprivileged, spoke out, blaming a few wealthy corporation farmers for adhering to a labor system long ago renounced by the rest of American industry. The Archbishop pointed out that even the rate of $1.25 an hour, recommended by many governmental agencies as a minimum fair wage for common laborers, adds up to a weekly salary on which it is "impossible to raise a family decently."

I was moved to tears at the Tucson conference. But the important thing is not that at one or two moments tears welled up in my eyes. The essential question is: why, in the light of the abject tragedy paraded before my vision, did I not weep with sorrow and anger from the first moment of the proceedings to the last? What is disturbing is not my tears but my insensitivity.

Perhaps the reader does not react emotionally to the abstract word "tragedy." Perhaps I should be specific. Perhaps I should tell of what I saw and heard recently when I traveled to the rich farming area centered at Oxnard, California.

At the Cabrillo Village labor camp in Saticoy, I met Mr. and Mrs. Manuel Robles and their three children. The Robles were in their mid-twenties. Their children were a six-year-old girl, a three-and-a-half-year-old boy, and a year-and-a-half-year-old girl. The family had arrived in Santa Paula on May 21, 1965, having come from Corpus Christi, Texas, where they had been recruited by the Delta Labor Agency.

The following day the father and mother became the victims of one of the abuses of the present system: the piecework basis; they were not paid an hourly wage, but given so much for each basket they turned in. They decided to ask a Mr. Besson, the manager of the grove, if they might be transferred to an area where the pickings were not so slim. Besson's reply was curt: "If you don't like it here, you can leave." Hurt by this attitude, and dismayed at their inability to make ends meet, the Robles decided to leave—thirteen days before their forty-five-day contract expired.

On the following day the Robles family trekked three hundred miles north, to San Jose. The man in charge of the farm labor office there made a number of telephone calls but was unable to find work for them, so they returned to the Oxnard area. A Mr. Bartolo Martinez was kind enough to let them stay at his home, even though he himself has a family of ten children and lives in a primitive shack scarcely large enough for a family of three. Robles was able to obtain work at the Saticoy Lemon Company, but the company refused to rent him a house, even though there were six or seven vacant shacks available. Robles was told only that the houses had already been rented. Two families had indeed moved in, but as of the date I talked to him—July 9—the other shacks were still empty. All this time Robles and his family had to live in their dilapidated car.

As if this were not bad enough, their young son became very ill with diarrhea and pneumonia. They took him to the Ventura General Hospital on Saturday, July 3, waited around the hospital grounds from eight o'clock at night until four the following morning, and then returned the next day. The hospital asked that the child be left there for at least three or four days.

The little boy's condition was not unusual. There was much sickness in the camp when I visited it, chiefly among infants. As public health officers can testify, the incidence of illness due to unsanitary conditions, exposure, and malnutrition is high in practically all farm labor camps.

The Robles family was by no means the only one in dire straits. In many instances migrant workers recruited from far away have been given false representation as to payment of transportation costs, wages, working and housing conditions, and the length of time for which employment is guaranteed.

In July the Emergency Committee to Aid Farm Workers, an organization of concerned citizens, learned of at least eleven family groups (recruited by the Delta Labor Agency in Texas and later employed at the Limoneira Ranch in Santa Paula) who had run into trouble. All the working members of these families had been either fired or forced to quit because of unsatisfactory wages, working conditions, or personal treatment. Seven of the families simply left the area but the remaining four were referred to the Emergency Committee by a sympathetic storekeeper in Santa Paula. They were totally without funds, stranded without future prospects of employment, and either evicted or under orders to vacate their houses at once. They had been warned that the skimpy paychecks due them would be withheld and utilities turned off unless they moved out.

All had been led to believe, in Texas, that they had been given contracts for ninety days of work and that their travel expenses would be returned to them at the end of that period. They had signed a form at the time of recruitment which seemed to them to guarantee these terms, but the form is not legally binding and not worth the paper it is printed on. By signing the form, the workers had agreed to a number of conditions, but there was no reciprocal signature on the part of the hiring agents or the prospective employer. Nor was there any indication of who had authorized the Delta Labor Agency to recruit workers, nor any identification by address or name of an authorized representative of the agency. In this one-sided "contract" the worker assumes all the risks and obligations. Nevertheless, on the basis of such a flimsy agreement, the eleven families had come west to California. In addition to the written "guarantees," they had been given oral assurances by the Delta Labor Agency representative who interviewed them that they could make up to $1.47 an hour and that they would have furnished houses plus free transportation. Some of them were told that the transportation costs would be deducted from their first two paychecks and returned to them after ninety days.

The Delta Labor man in Texas told the women that they would work in row crops: lettuce, strawberries, and asparagus. But when they arrived in California, all were put to work in citrus; the women were made to carry their own ladders in the orchards and to pick the tops of the trees, a maneuver far more dangerous than ground work. The "furnished" houses had nothing more than dogeared cots and a stove. I peered into the windows of some of the shacks; people had fashioned makeshift tables and chairs out of crates and boxes from the fields.

Some of the workers had been told the houses would be theirs to occupy at no charge, but as it turned out they had to pay fifty-five cents a day plus the cost of utilities.

Two of the workers fell from ladders while working, but received no medical attention, nor were accident reports filed as required.

The promises concerning wages proved empty. Some received $1.25 for the first forty-eight hours and then went on the piecework basis. When they complained about being given trees that would not yield even a dollar an hour (as had the Robles), they were told to pick up their checks and get out. Women who refused to climb ladders to the tops of the taller trees were summarily fired.

Some of the families had made the trip in their own cars. Others had to travel in a bus provided by the "company." Those who rode the buses said that the driver would stop only every eight hours or so, in violation of the state law that a public carrier transporting human beings must stop every *two* hours!

II

Such tragic stories are legion in the fields. A courageous man named Fred Van Dyke could tell of many more. Van Dyke is a board member of the National Advisory Committee on Farm Labor. For sixteen years he farmed in the San Joaquin Valley of California until his fellow growers hounded him out of the industry because his views became too civilized for them to tolerate. Van Dyke delivered an unforgettable declaration of humanitarian concern in October, 1960, in a speech before the Stockton Council of Churches: "As a citizen of this democratic country, as a Christian, simply as a human being, my conscience was increasingly troubled over the years by the evidence I saw of basic human damage to the men, women, and children who cultivate and harvest the crops in San Joaquin County where I farm. Let me give you just one example of the human damage which has forced me to look into my own conscience. Not too long ago, I noticed a farm worker's car parked beside the road, not more than a mile and a half from where I live. Do you know what I found inside that stifling car? Three little children. The youngest, a baby not more than a year old, was screaming from *pain*. The flesh on the lower part of his body was raw because he had diarrhea and had been soiling himself all day without being cleansed or changed. The next oldest, a youngster about three or four years old, was burning with the highest *fever* I have ever felt in any child—and I know something about children, because my wife and I have *six* of our own. The third child was a little boy of perhaps five or six. He was *unconscious* and very nearly *dead*. Would you like to know why those children were in that car? Would you like to know what the parents were doing? The parents were in a nearby orchard, picking cherries so that Americans could enjoy that luxury fruit at their breakfast tables, or on top of their banana splits, or in their Manhattan cocktails.

"No system can be tolerated within which such things

are possible. I do not care what arguments the Associated Farmers and Farm Bureau may advance. They complain about a 'cost-price squeeze.' They claim that agriculture is 'unique' because it deals with perishable commodities. They complain about the unpredictability of the weather. All this is so much *rationalization* and *evasion*. All of it is irrelevant when compared to even one single child weeping from hunger or from pain. The moral argument, the humanitarian argument, closes debate without any further evidence required. The argument based upon conscience demands—and I say *demands*—that existing arrangements in agricultural labor be rethought and rebuilt from the very ground up. The question of how this is to be done is secondary. The first step is to recognize that it *must* be done. Then ways will be found. If you agree with me that man is, at least when he has to be, capable of reason, then you will agree with me that things which must be done *can* be done."

In a way Van Dyke's message was prophetic. In 1965, a baby left in a car while its parents toiled in these same lush delta fields choked to death on its own vomit.

Dr. Hector Garcia, a Corpus Christi physician, has spoken out eloquently about those of his patients who are farm workers' children: "The children of migrant parents are born into a world completely of their own. An anemic mother, and possibly a tubercular father—a life that will take him into his world where he may possibly die within one year, either from diarrhea, tuberculosis, or malnutrition. His infancy would be a very close association with his brothers and sisters. Their home would be a one- or two-room shack with no inside running water and no flush toilets.

"If he lives to be of school age, he could possibly go to many schools on different occasions at different places, but will never average more than three years of schooling in his lifetime. His future life will be one of wandering, poverty, and more sickness. . . .

"I am still haunted by that remembrance of a day ten years ago when a little boy came to my office to ask me to go and see his mother, who was sick. I went to his home—a one-room shack. I found a dead mother with six children lying in the same bed, all covered with blood from the hemorrhage of a dying tubercular mother."

These sins cry to heaven. Not for vengeance but for attention. To those whose philosophies do not embrace the concept of an afterlife, the point may be of only poetic interest. But it should be of profound importance to those conservatives who profess Christianity yet seem inured to social injustice.

III

To be poor in the United States is almost certainly to be assured not only of second-rate medical attention but of a terribly inadequate education. A not unusual situation prevails in the Roosevelt Elementary School District No. 66 in the southern "fringe" area of metropolitan Phoenix. Despite the city's wealth there has been a shortage of classroom space for at least twenty years, with large numbers of pupils attending on a part-time basis. Many have been on a part-time schedule from the first to the fourth or fifth grades, thus losing the equivalent of a full year or more during the most critical learning period of their lives.

Education is, in fact, a vital target of the War on Poverty, and I am not referring now to the education of the poor but to the education of the rich and the middle class—of those whose apathy and opposition block the path to progress.

Father Joseph da Lio, a Spanish-speaking priest who works with migrants in the Dayton–Walla Walla, Washington, area, where string beans and peas are grown, has stressed the need for aid to migrant children and observed that if such children are not properly educated now, they will be social and economic problems for the community in later years. They might be termed "involuntary dropouts," since they will pose the same liabilities.

An eight-year-old migrant child has written in an essay this picture of what farm labor looks like: "Get down on your knees. Then start picking beans. When you get two hampers full, then you weigh them. After you weigh them, you put them on the truck. But before you put the beans on the truck, you put them in a sack. You must pick beans all day. You go home when the man tells you."

If the reader has difficulty feeling the appropriate empathy for the child's plight, I suggest that he imagine his own eight-year-old son or daughter as the principal player in the drama.

There is a nagging paradox to the vicissitudes of farm labor. California, for example, is the richest agricultural state in the Union, a garden of plenty so lush that it quite possibly could feed the entire country in an emergency. Yet the suffering of its agricultural workers is spectacular and pervasive. The heat in central and southern California during the summer months is desert-like and crushing. When I went through infantry basic training at Camp Roberts, near San Luis Obispo, in 1943, it was not uncommon to see strong, healthy young soldiers keel over in the midafternoon sun after a five-mile hike or a climb up a hillside packing a machine gun. Excessive loss of body fluids due to the heat made it necessary for our companies to be followed by KP squads carrying large canvas bags of pure, cool water and supplies of salt tablets. California's farm workers may toil up to twelve hours a day in temperatures soaring over a hundred degrees. No one provides them with cool, pure water or salt tablets. Often there are no sanitary drinking water facilities at all. Sometimes large open barrels of tepid water are there; sometimes the laborers must drink irrigation-ditch water.

Rev. Jack Mansfield has noticed that during the intense heat of summer, workers are frequently sick at the close of the day from dehydration and mineral imbalance. When a doctor told him that the workers should be taking salt tablets, Rev. Mansfield offered to furnish the tablets himself if the grower would supervise their distribution in order to prevent overdoses. The grower flatly refused.

The wanton disregard for the physical safety of fieldworkers would appall an industrial safety engineer. Women and children teeter at the top of tall ladders. Men, women, and even children operate the roaring mechanical monsters that pick some crops, this despite laws prohibiting minors from operating or being close to machinery. It goes on in spite of the grim evidence of some *five hundred injured and mangled children each year*. No wonder agriculture ranks as one of our most hazardous industries, with a death rate exceeded only by construction and mining.

But heat and machinery are not the only dangers. Nights in the valleys, plains, and deserts of the Southwest and Southeast can be bitter cold.

In February of 1959, when the National Advisory Committee on Farm Labor held public hearings in Washington, D.C., a Florida minister, the Rev. K. P. Thornton, journeyed at his own expense to appeal for his destitute parishioners: "Most camps are dilapidated shacks, with large families living in one room with no windows. The toilet facilities are the outside privy type that are so filthy many use the ground. The water supply is outside faucets with no water in the dwellings. Why should little children be forced to live in such filthy surroundings just because they were born in a migrant family?

"There is no way to heat the dwellings and bedding is not provided. In cold weather there is much suffering and we have supplied blankets to many of them. . . .

"Last winter, when all the crops were frozen and there was little or no work for over three months, we had many appeals for medical aid. We took them to county authorities and were sent from one agency to another until we were worn out, and in some cases paid the bill ourselves. Finally we were told that there was a provision whereby some of the expense was paid by the state. There is no place where the migrant can go for help and know that he's going to get it."

Insidiously, the animallike living conditions of the fields can, in the opinion of some public health officials, reach as far as the consumer's dinner table. There are no toilets for the workers in many fields. One grower who

is not altogether an anomaly ruled out field toilets because workers would lose time going to them; in many
instances the workers are forced to urinate and defecate
in the open fields, an eventuality which is not only
humiliating to themselves but potentially deadly.

The abuses against humanity which I have cited are
not rare. George Werner, of the U. S. Department of
Labor, investigated the Oxnard episode in which the
eleven families had been lured west under false pretenses.
He interviewed the heads of the families that were still
available, at considerable length. It is his opinion that
the Oxnard incident was by no means isolated.

The Emergency Committee to Aid Farm Workers be-
lieves that the experience of the eleven families has been
duplicated hundreds of times all over the state. Indeed
such instances are so frequent as to suggest a deliberate
deprecation of farm workers intended to discourage them,
the purpose being to support the growers' contention
that the domestic force is inherently unstable and un-
reliable. This is a canard the majority of growers hope to
pass off, to justify the importation of hordes of cheap
foreign labor.

But it is a canard that goes hand in hand with poverty.
One important reason for the uniqueness of Southwestern
poverty is the common fifteen-hundred-mile border with
a nation whose economic standards are at least thirty
years behind our own. This means that many thousands
of immigrants every year seek and attain permanent resi-
dence in the United States, and many more braceros and
border-jumping "wetbacks" come in temporarily, bloat-
ing the farm labor force. With such a pool of cheap labor
close at hand, Southwestern growers have found it possi-

ble to fend off American workers who require a higher
wage.

Beyond the purely economic factor, there is the serious
problem of racial, religious, and ethnic prejudice which
troubles the poor even when they apply for nonfarm jobs
for which they are qualified.

One speaker at the Tucson conference put it straight
from the shoulder: "Job discrimination is really the worst
kind of discrimination. If you don't want me in your
country club, it may be that I didn't want to go there in
the first place, and in any event, I have my own places
where I can gather with my friends. If you don't want
me in your restaurant, it is always possible for me to eat
elsewhere. But when you make it impossible for me to
get a good job, on the basis of the color of my skin, you
have struck at my dignity as a human being and at the
security of my family."

3 BLIGHT IN THE SOUTHWEST
I

How did these extremes of wealth and poverty come to be? What must be done to achieve a more humane balance? For the answers we must go back into the story of the early Southwest.

California, Arizona, New Mexico, Texas, and Nevada have had a history unlike that of other parts of the nation. The Indians, of course, were the original inhabitants. Their days became numbered when the first Spanish adventurers arrived seeking gold and other riches. Had the church not dispatched missionaries to accompany the conquistadores, it is likely the Indians would have like the buffalo been exterminated in the areas under Spanish control. The padres set up the missions that still stand, thus giving the Indians some indication that the

European intruders had interests above and beyond pillage, gold, slave-taking, rape, and domination.

For three centuries there was considerable interbreeding between the Spanish and the native Indians. Today a person referred to as Mexican may be pure Spanish, pure Indian, or have mixed Spanish-Indian blood.

The Spanish-speaking peoples of the Southwest are different from the Spanish-speaking colonies in other sections of the United States. With the American Indian they have shared defeat in war, concentration in isolated enclaves, and an unsought American citizenship. Like those of the Indians, their personal and property rights, which were legally guaranteed by a treaty, were ignored before the ink on the paper was dry. Unlike the Indians, whose misery they have shared, they have never had even the nominal protection of an agency such as the Bureau of Indian Affairs.

As Spain's power crumbled, the Spanish-Americans were left defenseless before the aggressive and expansion-minded Anglo-American settlers; hence, they were never able to organize meaningful resistance. Their lands were taken from them; they were treated as inferiors, and, for the most part, were left in the clutches of extreme poverty. Sister Blandina Segale, a Catholic Sister of Charity, has written in her book *At The End Of the Santa Fe Trail*: "In the early years of Anglo settlement in New Mexico the unsuspicious and naïve Spanish Americans were victimized on every hand. When the men from the states came out west to dispossess the poor natives of their lands, they used many subterfuges. One was to offer the owner of the land a handful of silver coins for the small service of making a mark on paper.

The mark was a cross which was accepted as a signature and by which the unsuspecting natives deeded away their lands. By this means many a poor family was robbed of all of its possessions."

The Anglo view that Indians and Spanish-Americans are inferior persists to this day. It is this attitude that lies at the heart of the matter, for when these guileless peoples were cast adrift by the rest of Southwestern society, the roots of poverty took hold.

II

Other ethnic groups people the Southwest today, including two million Negroes. Still the dominant group is the Anglo white. But he also is found in the lowest-income strata.

One thing I learned at the Tucson conference was that each of these groups has its own social problems. For example, the difficulty the Indian faces when he leaves the reservation is adjusting, even in these modern times, to a foreign environment. It is not merely the relatively common difficulty of moving from the country to the city, but rather it is learning to live in a fundamentally strange cultural environment. It is as if a resident of a sixteenth-century English village were suddenly dropped into twentieth-century Manhattan. The newcomer from the past would not only be quaintly anachronistic, but would speak a strange dialect as well.

There is presently much unrest in the Indian community. One Indian woman at the conference angrily exclaimed: "The [Indian] Commissioner—as far as I'm concerned—is a very good dodger. He doesn't answer his mail, he just refers letters to other people. We don't want to hear from other people. If we write to him, we want to hear from *him*. My life has been nothing but a life of promises. For 120 years we Indians have heard promises . . . not one of which has been kept! The Indian Bureau has never done one thing for me."

Such outbursts were common. Some of the poor spoke with controlled outrage at the indignity they had been made to suffer in a society presumably prepared to go to nuclear war over the principle that the dignity of the individual is of the most profound importance.

There was a pervading sense of frustration, of impatience with the status quo.

There seemed to be a general awareness on the part of the underprivileged that the dominant powers in the community had in the past not responded to their obligation even to study the background of the problem. Even Southwestern universities have avoided their responsibilities.

Although there are rich opportunities for social, cultural, and economic research, there are few other states where such scant sociological research is taking place. Colleges and universities generally have given slight encouragement to research into the causes of the serious economic and cultural problems that trouble the border states. Programs of research in the physical sciences there are aplenty. But there is little work concerned with improving the daily life of Southwestern citizens. The paradox, therefore, remains: a grubby hand-to-mouth existence (for it is no more than that) of millions, in a land of incomparable beauty and abundance.

III

One factor that makes the problem of poverty in the Southwest unique is the dominance of the nouveau riche. The lack of any true aristocratic "society" has created a culture in which the survival-of-the-fittest is the rule. Many citizens, still clawing their way up the ladder, are so interested in accumulating their own nest egg that it apparently rarely occurs to them to take a serious interest in the welfare of their less fortunate neighbors. Philanthropy, in the sense in which it is known in the Northern and Eastern sections of the country, is quite rare and tends to be limited to such "uncontroversial" fields as medicine, music, art, and the endowment of university chairs.

The degree of social progressivism which was achieved in, say, Boston, Philadelphia, New York, or Chicago forty years ago has yet to be achieved in the Southwest. One of the many reasons this is true is that those religious denominations which tend to inspire social progressivism —Jews, Quakers, Universalists-Unitarians, liberal Catholics, and the more socially prestigious Protestant groups —find themselves outnumbered in the Southwest by the numerous fundamentalist sects. Amazingly, Arizona voters as late as 1964 were faced with an evolution-teaching abolition measure on the ballot. The state is one of the few where anti-union "right to work" laws are on the books.

There does seem to be at long last a growing public awareness of the destitution and squalor in which Indians and Negroes live in the Southwest. But at the same time the living conditions of Mexican-Americans has been termed by Robert Choate of Tucson "America's best kept secret."

Choate's description of the situation is startling. "Education for the indigent," he says, "is haphazard in these areas. Health measures are shocking. Birth rates are high but so are infantile deaths and tuberculosis. Vocational training is often unknown, day-care centers are practically unheard of. Recreation is marginal. Incentive is absent. Crime is high. . . . Social concern at a low ebb. Public welfare policies are brutal, shallow, suspicion-laden, and restrictive."

Another factor that perpetuates poverty in the midst of plenty in the Southwest is the traditionally weak communication between the power elite and the leaders of the handicapped ethnic groups. Nor is communication between the typical Anglo social-volunteer and the impoverished much better. Again and again at the President's conference I heard the theme that meaningful dialogue between the poor and those entrusted with helping them is lacking. There were repeated recommendations that one way to build bridges was to hire more qualified Mexicans, Indians, and Negroes, to work *within the welfare structure itself.*

Tremendous applause rocked the committee room when one speaker asked, "Who will control these new anti-poverty programs at the local level? The same individuals who have for so long been giving it the wrong kind of treatment?"

Much of the testimony dealt with the problem of the underpaid farm worker. I am convinced that if the American people ever get a clear picture of the pitiful state of the hundreds of thousands of men, women, and children who compose our farm labor force, they will demand remedial action, and fast.

Years ago manufacturers paid shamefully low wages to exploited workers in cruel sweatshops. But this lasted only until the spotlight of public attention was focused on the situation. The American people, shocked at the disclosures of inhuman working conditions, demanded that workers be treated like human beings. It has been thirty years and more since we legislated ourselves basic standards of minimum security: minimum wages, unemployment compensation, the right to organize and bargain collectively, adequate prohibitions against child labor. But we still refuse to give these to the farm worker.

Why was he overlooked? Perhaps because he was invisible. The citizen of earlier years could not avoid seeing the evils of the sweatshops because they existed in the cities, under his nose. But the citizen of today cannot see, as Michael Harrington has observed, what goes on across the nation in out-of-the-way rural areas. Here are the blue-sky sweatshops.

Consequently we find it hard to believe that hundreds of thousands of our fellow citizens wander about in poverty, living in tarpaper shacks, chicken coops, tents, or under the stars. Dr. Paul O'Rourke, California's Anti-Poverty Chief, has called Highway 99, stretching from the Sacramento Valley in the north to the Imperial Valley in the south, "the longest slum in the world." But the farm workers' shacks and shanties which border it are set back from the highway, out of sight of the tourists blithely speeding from one vacation attraction to another.

The migrant farm worker is an unknown stranger, without a substantial home, without a vote, without friends, without a future. Farm families still seem to be re-enacting the most depressing scenes from *Tobacco Road* and *The Grapes of Wrath.*

As for the chances of the migrant or semimigrant getting unemployment insurance or other benefits of enlightened legislation, he might as well hail from Mars. He has been systematically excluded from almost all social and labor legislation. In 1961, California permitted him disability insurance, but it comes out of his thin pocket. Some laws have been passed for the protection of the migrant and his children but they are mostly inadequate and frequently ignored.

The challenge to the American people is plain. In a nation which prides itself on being both the most humane in the world—and is certainly the most prosperous—the continued impoverishment of farm workers is neither morally nor economically justified.

4 AGRIBUSINESS: THE CORPORATE FARMER

Thus far I have talked about the American farm worker in terms of his impoverished lot, his bleak day-by-day existence, his forlorn future. Because he is treated like the dirt in which he grovels for a living, it might seem that he is an inconsequential spare cog in a smoothly functioning machine. But in fact he is a key part of the field-to-table process, an indispensable man in an industry that rings up billions of dollars a year in receipts. Why is he the forgotten man in the march of progress that has made American agriculture the most productive in the world? Forgotten even though it is claimed he is in short supply? The answer is bound up in the evolution of American agriculture from the individual family farm to the huge corporate land complex.

Until the era of World War I, the family farm was the stereotype of American agriculture. Its modest acreage was tended by the farmer and his sons, aided at harvest-time by a few hired hands. Symbolized by the windmill, the hand pump, the plow, and the red barn, it survives today largely in the popular imagination.

Eventually, revolutionary technical developments were introduced to farming which brought about radical change. Rapid refrigerated freight-car and truck transportation facilities, chemical preservatives, and food-freezing techniques made it possible for farmers to specialize in otherwise perishable crops and market them under more effectively controlled conditions. As growers discovered greater profits in individual, specialized crops, they switched over most of their acreage to them. This meant that the harvest season could no longer be spread over a major part of the year. There was a very busy planting season followed in time by a hectic harvest season, with periods of relative leisure in between. As agriculture moved inexorably in the direction of specialization, requiring large quotas of farm workers in certain places at certain times, the roots of the present farm labor problem took hold.

Revolutionary developments were also occurring in the factories that manufactured farm machinery. Powerful tractors pulling large plows, cultivators, and harvesters, as well as advances in methods of fertilization and irrigation, led to higher yields per acre with less physical effort and smaller labor requirements. *Fortune* magazine in June, 1955, sketched the change: "The most important development in the history of American agriculture, by all odds, has been the spectacular way its productivity has been improved in the last quarter century. Thanks to a fertile progressive technology, the average U.S. farm worker is 110 per cent more productive than he was twenty-five years ago, and so 37 per cent fewer farm workers, putting in fewer hours, are producing 50 per cent more than U.S. agriculture produced twenty-five years ago."

One aspect of this agricultural revolution has been the accelerating trend toward the merger of small farms into larger ones. There has been an evolution toward fewer and larger farms, and a corresponding increase in the share of the total agricultural output for which the mammoth farms, ranches, and orchards are responsible. (The old image of the individual farmer endures for the simple reason that for thousands of years it was the only image. Even today, simple peasant farmers comprise more than two thirds of the population of our planet. Seventy per cent of the nearly three billion living humans are occupied in farming in one form or another. It is primarily in the United States that farming has changed so drastically.)

Agriculture has simply followed the trend of other American industries toward consolidation, bigness, and domination by the few. To identify the corporate complex, which so closely resembles the rest of U.S. industry, the descriptive term "agribusiness" has been coined. The enormous farms and ranches of agribusiness, some encompassing thousands of acres, are corporately owned, often by absentee landlords, groups of investors, or holding companies. Surprisingly, such companies as Standard Oil and the Southern Pacific Railroad are heavily involved in agribusiness through their farmland holdings. A vast amount of acreage is owned or leased by such integrated field-to-supermarket giants as the California Packing Corporation and Stokely-Van Camp.

It has been said that the strings of California's $3.6-billion-a-year agribusiness are pulled from the redwood-paneled offices on San Francisco's Montgomery Street, the Wall Street of the West. In addition to growers, packers, processors, middlemen, and distributors, agribusiness embraces allied enterprises such as banks (the Bank of America, the world's largest, is the prime financer of California farms), shipping and transportation companies, land companies (Kern County Land Company, for all practical purposes, *is* Kern County), and utilities, plus other large corporations which have a stake in the prosperity of the field-to-table process.

The anatomy of this "giant octopus," as one packing company executive put it, can be seen by studying the interlocking directorships of the agribusiness corporations. Packing executives sit on the boards of directors of banks and land companies. Bankers who trade in farm loans proliferate on the boards of packing and land companies. Realty executives who deal in farm acreage sit on the boards of shipping and packing companies. The labyrinth goes on and on.

As a group agribusiness executives are hardheaded and dollar-orientated, which is by way of saying they are not much different from executives in other fields. The tremendous technological advances of agriculture are all to their credit, but where they differ from executives in other fields is in their archaic concept of their responsibility to human beings.

An admirable exception is Norton Simon, chief execu-

tive of Hunt Foods and Industries, the nation's largest
tomato processor. A man of broad horizons who is an
art connoisseur and a regent of both the huge University
of California and the tiny liberal Reed College of Port-
land, Oregon, Simon not long ago expressed his version
of the function of a modern corporation: "We are beyond
the day and age of the need of capitalism for survival.
We need it for only one thing—the betterment of the
human being. Certainly we have a lot more than we can
eat, haven't we?"

As with other industrial interests, agribusiness main-
tains well-financed lobbies to foster public sympathy and
promote favorable legislation. The late James P. Mitch-
ell, Secretary of Labor under Eisenhower, spoke bluntly
of the power of the agribusiness lobby. The effort is
spearheaded by the conservative American Farm Bureau
Federation, which is active on Capitol Hill. Various state
and regional groups lobby within their sphere of in-
fluence. The Council of California Growers, for example,
represents the large growers who supply the packers, food
chains, and marketing cooperatives. The State Board of
Agriculture, which has a hand in setting agricultural
policy, is overwhelmingly grower-dominated. The pattern of tightly organized agribusiness lobbies is repeated
in other agricultural states.

There is a mistaken impression that agribusiness speaks
for the American farmer, and that the farm labor problem is a burden shared by *all* U.S. farmers. Actually the
problem belongs almost exclusively to agribusiness, which
rules those crops requiring large quantities of seasonal
labor: cotton, vegetables, and fruits. About 54 per cent of
all farms hire no labor whatsoever. On 41 per cent of the

farms the farmer and members of his family do practically all the work. *Five per cent of the farms pay three quarters of the nation's farm wages and they are the huge farms of agribusiness.*

The agricultural revolution has found the small farmer sitting on the opposite side of the fence from agribusiness. In trying to get a fair price for his food and fiber, he is bucking the same powerful bloc that the farm laborer fights in trying to get a fair wage. When the small farmer goes to market, buyers do not bid for his produce. The buyer from one large packing or processing firm offers the same low price as the buyer from another—take it or leave it.

Protest against such unfree-enterprise collusion is drowned out by the clamor of such other "farmers" as the Kern County Land Company, which owns 2800 square miles of land in fourteen states, an empire *twice the size of Rhode Island;* Standard Oil, which holds more than 218,000 acres in Southern California; the Southern Pacific, which claims 201,000 acres in the same region; the Tejon Ranch in Southern California with its approximately 315 square miles, about the size of New York City's five boroughs.

The American Farm Bureau Federation is the voice of agribusiness, while the National Farmers Union, as the voice of the small farmer, seeks to preserve the fast-dwindling family farm.

Formed in 1902, near the little town of Point, Texas, by a handful of men worried about low farm prices and the bleak future in prospect for those living *on* the land, the NFU has sided with farm workers in advocating, among

Poverty and People

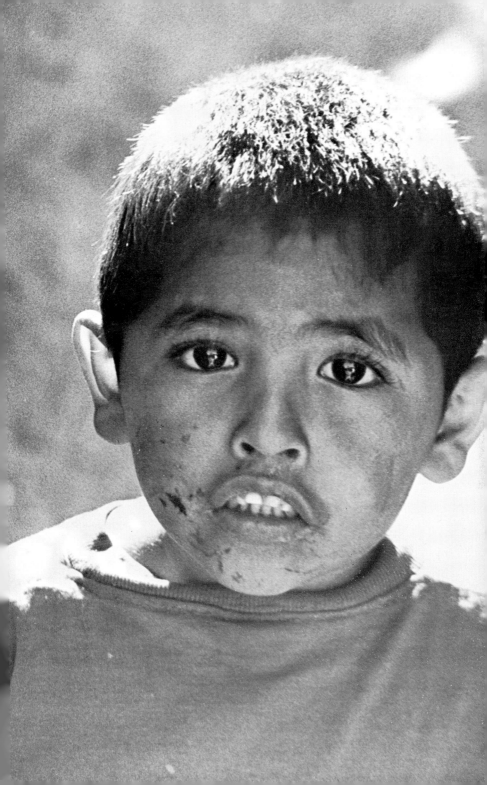

other things, extension of the Fair Labor Standards Act to agriculture.

Although agribusiness has justified paying low wages by protesting that it is caught in a "cost-price squeeze," in reality it is the small farmer who is being strangled by spiraling costs and fixed market prices because he is at the mercy of the food industry. The dominant factor in the economic life of farmers is the grocery chain. These chains, with their power to manipulate prices, have control of a farm commodity from the farm point of production to the shopping bag. If present trends continue, competition in the marketplace may be eliminated. A reduction of farmers to sharecroppers or farm workers who have lost all control over farm management could follow.

The National Commission on Food Marketing, chaired by Phil S. Gibson, retired chief justice of the California Supreme Court, and including Senators Warren Magnuson, Roman Hruska, Philip Hart, and Gale McGee, has conducted an exhaustive probe of the situation. Its report will be in President Johnson's hands shortly.

The Commission has listened to testimony outlining the ruthless tactics sometimes resorted to in order to whip small farmers into line. Harry L. Graham, a spokesman for the National Grange, cited one ugly instance: "A well-known food chain moved five carloads of potatoes into the grocery stores on the eastern shore of Lake Michigan and sold them at substantial reductions in order to break the potato market at Benton Harbor, Michigan, at the time they were ready to purchase potatoes."

Graham declared the same technique had been used with beef cattle, strawberries, and other crops. Although some farmers' cooperatives have been able to "eliminate economic aggression," he went on, self-defense is not always possible. "There have been some rather unsavory reports from farmers of blacklisting and of extreme difficulty in terms of financing farm operations," he said. One of these involved Arkansas poultrymen who attempted to organize but were beaten back by a boycott set up by several corporations, including one of the country's largest feed and grain processors, an affair under investigation by the U. S. Department of Agriculture. Graham proposed as an antidote collective bargaining by small farmers in the same manner as organized labor; this, he said, was the only feasible way to protect the market and combat blacklisting and boycotts.

Collective bargaining, the strength of unity, does seem to be the only weapon available to the humble man at the bottom of the heap, be he farmer or laborer. We have learned from experience the results of leaving people to the tender mercies of an industry in headlong pursuit of the dollar; yet we have done so in agriculture because we have believed in the myth that agribusiness is *different* from other industries. Supported by this subterfuge, agribusiness has been able to claim special privilege—the license to import foreign workers to man its factories of the field.

5 MYTH OF THE BRACERO
I

Imagine, if you will, Big Steel importing as the nucleus of its work force Polish steelworkers willing to work at little more than Iron Curtain wages. Imagine the electronics industry bringing in cadres of patient Japanese assembly-line workers at subpar Oriental wages. Imagine the various manufacturing and construction industries importing in wholesale lots unskilled and semiskilled workers from impoverished countries, eager to toil for a pittance. All of this with the stamp of approval—and helping hand—of the United States government.

The result would be chaos. American workers would be forced to grovel for what job crumbs were left. The unemployment rate would soar, wage levels would tumble. The outflow of currency caused by remittances of the

foreign workers to their home countries would put a
further strain on our dwindling gold reserves. Low wages
would shrink buying power. With the demand for goods
and services ebbing, local merchants would be in distress.
The velocity of the dollar would be braked and the economy would stagger.

Fortunately such a thing can not happen in twentieth-
century America because mass importation of labor is
outlawed. Outlawed, that is, except for one industry:
agribusiness. Under the aegis of the government, agribusiness has brought in droves of braceros—the hard-
working Mexican farmhands—to harvest its crops. On a
diminished scale, the consequences mentioned above *have*
happened. American farm workers have time and again
been rebuffed by growers staffed with braceros; they have
been forced to scramble for intermittent work or go on
relief. Wages are depressed below the rest of industry—
below the level of decency. At the height of the bracero
program, millions of dollars a year left the country, creating a drain against which President Johnson has coun-
seled. In the agricultural hubs—Brawley, California, in
the Imperial Valley is a good example—small merchants
have been hard-hit. Community life, too, has been stunted,
because the bracero is not a permanent member of the
community nor a participant in its economic and cultural
life.

Agribusiness staked its claim to the services of the
bracero on the grounds that an assured labor supply is
absolutely essential to the timely harvesting of perishable
crops. It contends that the American worker is, alter-
natively: indolent, incapable, unable to withstand the

MYTH OF THE BRACERO 53

rigors of the field, unpredictable, unstable, more disposed toward government largesse than toward a hard day's work—or just not there. Hence the dire need for willing Mexican nationals. Not mentioned is the obvious fact that the bracero is a cheap labor windfall.

One key to the issue of braceroism lies in the long tradition of imported and subjugated labor in American agriculture. Before passage of the immigration laws of 1916, American farmers depended each year on a fresh supply of European immigrants for temporary and seasonal help. At various times in our history, farmers in the Western states assumed they had a permanent migratory labor force in the flood of Chinese, Japanese, and Hindus originally brought in to build railroads and push the frontier westward. These unfortunates were dumped into labor pools to be tapped at the growers' pleasure under gentlemen's agreements regulating wages and conditions. Eventually most of the Orientals and Europeans found permanent work in the cities or took up farming on a modest scale at the earliest possible moment.

After the turn of the century, passage of the Chinese Exclusion Act tended to dry up the pools. They were gradually refilled by a steady immigration of Mexicans to the border states. A rural people to begin with, overawed by the mystique of the great country *del Norte*, they clustered in Spanish-speaking enclaves and formed a willing core of the farm labor force. Their ranks were bolstered by wetbacks, who due to their illegal status were agreeable to the most servile conditions. The indigent Mexicans provided, in the truest sense, what George Santayana called one of the most crucial raw materials of industry: man.

II

In the thirties a large segment of the migratory work force was composed of displaced persons from Oklahoma, Arkansas, Missouri, and Texas who were deprecatingly referred to as "Okies." These were the Dust Bowl refugees who swept westward to Arizona and California in long bedraggled caravans. During the Great Depression they grabbed at whatever straws they could find, but most later resettled in their native areas or moved to more promising ones. Today the Okies are a decided minority in the migratory work force, remembered with sorrow in Steinbeck's *The Grapes of Wrath*. Ironically a number of Okies have become prosperous landowners in California, a state which once dispatched armed guards to bar them from its borders.

The chaos and tragedy of the Dust Bowl days forms a backdrop to the present predicament. For decades the Great Plains lying between the Mississippi and the Rockies had been unwisely farmed. Cattle and sheep overgrazed the land; farming methods that gave no heed to conservation compounded the damage to the soil. In the Depression year 1932 a great drought hit the region, and by late the following year dust storms turned the countryside into a semidesert. Prairie farmers were forced into tenancy at the rate of some 40,000 a year. Eventually the bankers who held farm mortgages took over vast portions of the territory, sent in bulldozers and tractors to remove the vestiges of tenant-farmer culture, and introduced methods of mass cultivation.

The human toll was high. Three out of every five Oklahoma farmers were tenants; every year 40 per cent of them would wander gypsylike to the West. Over a four-year period, more than 300,000 farm refugees entered California in battered automobiles laden with their pathetic belongings. These were not bums or winos or drifters. They were people who had belonged to the land, who had drawn their existence from it, and now were simply no longer able to do so. It is a shameful chapter in the history of California that in 1935 and 1936 the Los Angeles Chamber of Commerce illegally attempted to repel the migrants by what was called a "Bum Blockade." Said a bitter farmer at the time: "When they need us, they call us *migrants*. After we pick the crops, we're *bums* and we've got to get out."

The living and working conditions imposed on the unfortunate Okies were deplorable and at times immoral. When they tried to strike for better wages and working conditions, farm interests retaliated with goon squads, tear gas, stool pigeons, spies, and vigilantes armed with pick handles.

It was in response to this outrage that in 1937 President Franklin D. Roosevelt's U. S. Farm Security Administration attempted to help by granting loans to tenant farmers, but the only aid that society was civilized enough to offer at the time was palliative. Although at one time the Farm Security Administration was assisting some 30,000 families in California alone, the root problem was never really solved. It was only with the coming of World War II and the huge manpower appetites of the defense plants that many of the migrants were able to leave the fields for decent and well-paying jobs.

III

It was the wartime manpower shortage which brought the first braceros to the United States to replace the Okies at the bottom rung of the socioeconomic ladder. John Zuckerman, of the California Growers Farm Labor Committee in Stockton, says: "In 1942, prior to conception of the Mexican labor program, our company lost 2700 acres of sugar beets (worth $175,000) because we could not obtain laborers to thin, weed, or harvest the crop. Three major sugar companies in California spent thousands of dollars trying to recruit workers from Mississippi and Arkansas. Several hundred unemployed were transported at growers' expense from these areas, with completely unsatisfactory results. (May I stress that this was at a time when we were at war and the whole world was crying out for food and fiber. . . .)

"At our own expense we hired several labor-procurement specialists to travel the country seeking workers with a guarantee of high pay and good living conditions. The results speak for themselves; the 2700 acres of sorely needed sugar beets were abandoned. Such wasteful and tragic experiences as this made clear the need for a dependable supplemental labor supply. So, late in 1942, the bracero program of importing Mexican nationals for short periods during peak seasons was inaugurated. Even though less than 27,000 workers were brought into California from Mexico in 1943 for short periods of supplemental work, not a single crop was lost. And since that date, whenever the bracero program has been in effect, not an acre of crops in California has been lost through lack of harvest labor."

Thus agribusiness had its foot in the door. And it was not about to take it out. Like many another wartime measure the bracero program did not die with the emergency.

True, workers were slow to return to the fields. Many had improved their lot with skills learned in the military. Many who had tasted higher wages and superior conditions in the defense industries were reluctant to return to the farm. Nor did the growers especially relish the return of prodigals tainted with ideas of unionism.

The shortage was not severe enough to warrant a sustained clamor for more braceros. But even in a year of recession and unemployment, almost 450,000 braceros were allowed into the United States. The growers had simply become used to a reservoir of cheap labor that was completely docile. The bracero, who had been justified as a supplementary worker, became the heart of the work force.

Indeed, the bracero, from the agribusiness viewpoint, was an ideal solution. Selectively recruited in the interior of Mexico by labor contractors, he invariably turned out to be a prime physical specimen with previous farm labor experience. His health was checked gratis by an accommodating U.S. government. For the duration of his stay he was under contract to the growers and indentured for his transportation. At the slightest sign of dissent, he could be shipped back to Mexico. He came alone and lived in crude barracks, obviating family or housing problems. He was a chattel, and a productive one at that. Under the stern control of the field boss, he worked like a dog. He was paid not on an hourly basis but on a piecework basis—so much per basket. Despite his awesome productivity he made only about *eighty cents an hour!* When he was no longer useful, he was sent back to Mexico with no strings attached.

During the postwar years the bracero program drifted along informally under the benevolent eyes of the United States and Mexican governments. A number of abuses crept into the system. Since the bracero was not part of an attached labor force, many growers looked upon him as a piece of machinery to be shuttled about as the need required. (The analogy is quite literal: some growers discarded machinery because they found the bracero cheaper to lease and operate.) As a result he was shoved into squalid barracks and shacks, fed unfit food (and charged for room and board), and given only minimal sanitary facilities and medical care. At times he was outrageously overcharged at the company store for the bare necessities of life. There were too many instances in which he was not given the amount of work specified in the contract. Field bosses had a habit of shaving the amount due him. Unscrupulous and unregulated labor contractors siphoned off percentages of his paychecks that would put a loan shark to shame. The reckless disregard for his well-being was typified by the dilapidated, over-crowded trucks and buses in which he was herded from field to field—without portal-to-portal pay.

The bracero himself was helpless in the face of these abuses. Illiterate, speaking a foreign language, he was a stranger on alien soil with no one to speak for him. He knew that standing up for his rights meant being whisked back to Mexico in disgrace. What adds to the desperately poor conditions in the bracero's homeland is the fact that he struggled mightily for the privilege of coming to the United States only to suffer this cruel treatment. For the poor rural Mexican, becoming a bracero was the goal of a lifetime. He was a hero in his community, one of the few who had ever traveled to the United States. For the honor, he was willing to pay what often amounted to his life savings to palms-up Mexican officials in order to obtain his clearance. When he returned home he was well heeled—in the relative terms of poverty.

In time, the Mexican government became sensitive to the exploitation of its nationals. It urged the United States to enact and enforce laws protecting the bracero. In 1951, when the Korean War precipitated another, less severe manpower shortage, Congress passed Public Law 78, which codified the bracero program. Provisions of Public Law 78 required growers to place in trust a percentage of the bracero's anticipated earnings, to abide by minimal standards of housing and food, to guarantee work for at least three quarters of the life of the contract, and to correct other areas of abuse. These provisions were at the same time humanitarian and cynical, for *they gave to the bracero a modicum of relief that had never been considered for the American worker.*

Enforcement of the provisions turned out to be token and perfunctory. Mariano Arevalo, a former federal compliance officer, told Los Angeles *Times* labor editor Ruben Salazar in 1963: "I got sick of it. Though I was supposed to see that braceros were protected under the law, pressure was always applied by growers and I was often instructed to 'take it easy.' After all, the bracero could not hurt me and the grower might."

Henry P. Anderson, former public health research assistant at the University of California, encountered similar dissuasion. In 1958 he was prevented from interviewing braceros at the El Centro staging compound operated by the U. S. Department of Labor, which administered the bracero program. When he handed in his report to the University, critical sections were suppressed, particularly a section on the power structure behind braceroism.

As Congressman Henry Gonzales of Texas has put it, braceros, through no fault of their own, have been "used to bring the misery of a people in one country to further depress the misery of a people in another country."

6 PARIAHS IN THE MIDST OF PLENTY

Public Law 78, formalizing the bracero program, was originally intended, as we have seen, to be a stopgap measure to tide agribusiness over the Korean emergency. Its life was stipulated at two years but, like the man who came to dinner, it stayed on and on. Through one excuse or another, the agribusiness lobby was able to obtain extension after extension, prevailing largely on the conservative Republican-Southern Democrat coalition in Congress. The excuses admittedly contained a nub of validity and were convincingly presented. But for the most part they were either grossly exaggerated or were smokescreens covering the simple reluctance of agribusiness to relinquish its privilege.

The principle argument of agribusiness is that its problems are unique because of harvesting's seasonal peaks and the perishability of the crop. Due to the critical timing element it needs an assured work force at the times and places required. The bracero—it is argued—fulfills this need; the domestic does not. One is tempted to suggest that the fishery and lumbering industries, to mention two other highly seasonal operations, would dearly love to bring in contingents of foreign workers. But those industries have somehow managed to attract a labor force that fills the bill year after year.

Agribusiness has been able to secure special treatment because it has succeeded in putting the cart before the horse. Public Law 78 clearly specified that braceros were to be allowed *only if sufficient domestic workers were unavailable.* In other words, the American was to be considered the core of the work force, the bracero the reserve. Agribusiness simply reversed the order: the domestic became second choice. Palmer Mendelson, San Francisco strawberry-asparagus processor, who gives frequent speeches from the growers' point of view, recently told *Ramparts* magazine: "The bracero is a professional —others are amateurs. You have to have a hard core of professionals who can be shifted with crop conditions."

What Mendelson possibly means by "professional" is that certain crops require a knack which can be acquired in time or learned in a few days of on-the-job training. Many domestic workers are "professionals"; the rest could be if the growers took the time to train them, as is the case in other industries.

At times the bracero labor forces have represented over 35 per cent of all seasonal farm workers in California.

Some crops became known as "dominated crops" because the Mexican nationals forced out the domestic workers. In a dominated crop the forces of the free labor market don't operate. Wages are merely administered.

As bracero domination continued, more and more American workers found themselves on the outside looking in. At a 1962 Labor Department hearing in Los Angeles, James Davis of Sacramento told of his experience: "Right after the bracero program started I went to the growers I had known for years and I tried to get myself a job on the tomatoes, the way I always had before. I remember going to Lindsay Cochran. He is one of the biggest growers in the area. He said, 'We're not using anybody but nationals this year.' The same thing happened to me many, many times during those ten years."

In so often playing second fiddle, the domestic worker naturally became disheartened. Stories are legion that the growers deliberately tried to discourage Americans, knowing that for every one who drifted away from the farm they could legally lay claim to one more bracero. For example, a grower would place an order with the farm placement office for, say, one hundred workers at daybreak the next morning. One hundred workers would show up in his field ready for work, some after driving long distances at their own expense. It would turn out that the grower actually needed only fifty. One of two things would happen: fifty would be turned away empty-handed, or all one hundred would only get in a half day's work—and receive a half day's pay. In fairness it must be said that growers are instinctively cautious when it comes to harvesting their crops, and since there is no penalty for overordering, they tend to hedge their bets at the worker's expense. But in many cases the overestimation was so flagrant and repetitive that it seemed to be by design rather than accident.

A depressed wage level was the only harvest American workers reaped from the bracero program. Art Hendricks of Hillmar, California, related the bitter yield at the Los Angeles hearings: "I remember in 1948, when they didn't have any braceros, we got a dollar-ten a bucket (for cherries) then . . . after they ran the nationals in, the price went down to eighty-five cents a bucket and even lower. Just the last couple of seasons, it finally got back up to where it was fourteen years ago: a dollar-ten a bucket. And the only reason it did was because the Union put the heat on the government and made them take out the nationals."

Manuel Juarez of Stockton, who said he had been a farm laborer since he was "six or seven years old," reported at the same hearings: "In 1950 and 1951 we made pretty good money picking tomatoes. We got twenty-six cents a box, and sometimes even more. That was before they got the braceros in the San Joaquin County. After they got them, the price went down.

"They used to treat us like human beings. When I was planting strawberries over in the Salinas Valley, I remember they used to give us a ten-minute break every two and a half hours, morning and afternoon, so we could take a smoke or whatever we wanted. No more breaks since the braceros. Water, same thing . . . I guess they figure braceros don't need rest and don't need water."

Raul Aguilar, who ran a small grocery store catering to farm workers, told the National Advisory Committee on Farm Labor why he had to go back to work in the fields: "Lettuce used to be picked by the local workers. The wages used to be twenty-five cents a box; sometimes a good worker used to make almost a hundred dollars a week, working seven days a week. Most of these people used to be our customers, and we made pretty good money. Soon these people found themselves out of jobs because the Mexican nationals started working in everything. They dry-packed lettuce in the fields at 82½ cents an hour and soon the local workers started to work fewer hours because the nationals did all the hourly work. Soon we had to close our grocery store because all our customers were out of work. We moved to Stockton, California, in 1955, starting all over again; working in the onions at ten cents a basket, picking tomatoes at thirteen to fourteen cents a [fifty-pound] box. . . ."

Listen to the revealing story of another displaced person of the fields: "I am Maria Moreno, forty years old, mother of twelve children. Born in Karnes City, Texas; raised in Corpus Christi. Since 1928, I start working in agricultural work. I been a worker all my life. I know how to handle a man's job like a man and I'm not ashamed to say it. I'm American citizen, and I'm talking for justice. Not only for me or for my family but all the migrant workers. We been suffering for so long. Waiting and hoping, but it seems like that our hope has been lost.

"Nineteen thirty-two, we're picking cotton in Texas, twenty-five cents a hundred. We're chopping cotton ten cents a row. And have to support the children who in those days did never know what shoes were on their foot. Our children didn't know that they have to drink milk every day. Our children eat meat once a week. We can't afford it.

"Nineteen forty, we came to California. Waiting and hoping to find . . . a better living condition for ourselves and for our family. The braceros came in. We had to move from the Imperial Valley. We hit Salinas. Here come the braceros. Well, we're tickled anyway when we work a little. We can feed our children. Half eat. The road became our home. The ground is our table. People think that because somebody else have something to eat, they think the whole world have some. The thing that really hurts me is this: that we are living in a rich America, that the people been sending food, the clothing overseas. And then forgotten us. That we are citizens, and we are living in America. That's what really hurts me, and I hope that you people help us do something for this situation. You won't have to go very far. You go travel a little up here to Mendota. Wooklake. Visalia. Firebaugh. Huron. All places around here. You find out. People sleeping on the floor for so long. . . .

"The ranchers say they don't make any money, but one thing I know for sure: they're lying. I never heard of a rancher go and knock at the welfare doors and ask for something to eat like the agricultural workers do.

"What I say it's the truth, and I'm not afraid to say it. For too long, the agricultural workers been afraid. When somebody holler, we jump. Well, I'm not afraid no more. I guess we got rights too. I guess we been suffering so much. It is time to ask for justice."

The simple probity of Mrs. Moreno's plea is summed up in her final word—"justice." Farm workers want justice, not charity. They want to place their services on the auction block in a free market, not a captive one. It is clear that the bracero program contributed to the poverty of seasonal farm workers. In our economic system an increasing supply of anything results in a lowered price. The same thing applies to labor. Farm groups preach the holy law of supply and demand but seek the abridgment of this law in regard to farm labor. Public Law 78 was obviously a government-supported alteration of the law of supply and demand on the farm labor market.

Under the bracero program, with simultaneous exclusion of American farm workers from the protection of most state and national labor laws, conditions for farm labor since the end of World War II steadily worsened. While most workers *improved* their living standards during the postwar years, the ratio of wages received by hourly paid farm workers *fell* from 54 per cent of the wages received by factory workers in 1948 to 46 per cent in 1956.

The Mexican contract-labor program was used to create a surplus of farm workers, thereby pressing wages down and compelling both domestic and foreign labor to accept substandard working conditions on a like-it-or-lump-it basis. After deliberately lowering wages offered to American workers to a point where the employers knew they were not acceptable, the growers then offered the inevitable "labor shortage" as the rationalization for importing Mexican nationals.

Whipsawed between the evils of the bracero program and the perversity of some growers, the American field-worker has been a pariah in the midst of plenty, a second-class citizen in a proud democracy.

No wonder he does not always respond when agribusiness snaps its fingers.

7 PHANTOMS IN THE FLESH

The plea of agribusiness that an acute shortage of domestic help makes the bracero program indispensable raises the age-old question: which came first, the chicken or the egg? By alienating the domestic work force, braceroism created what shortage there may be—a shortage which, it has been shown time and time again, miraculously disappears when decent wages and conditions are offered. Because of braceroism, wages hit rock bottom and working conditions did not even begin to keep pace with other industries. Farm work fell into low repute, became a last resort. A man had to be desperate to engage in it: a stigma became attached to it. Two former braceros who later were able to immigrate to the United States and obtain construction jobs through the hod carriers' union echoed the refrain: "Farm work? That's pretty low!"

In 1963, a foreman told a Los Angeles *Times* reporter why farm work is looked down upon: "You see those braceros? The rate for picking those pear tomatoes is twenty-five cents a box. This crop isn't too good, so they're not picking more than two and one-half or three boxes an hour.

"Say they work the usual ten hours a day at this rate. They'd be making $32.50 to $37.50 a five-day week. But because these men are braceros they're assured at least $1 an hour under international agreement. So they'll make at least $50 a five-day week. Not the domestic, though. He's not protected by a minimum wage law and must pick this crop at sixty to seventy-five cents an hour. A domestic would make $32.50 to $37.50 a five-day week on this crop—not $50 like the bracero. You see why the domestic will not pick these tomatoes?"

The domestic simply cannot afford to work at bracero levels, much less below them. The average income of American farm workers is at the disgraceful level of $1500 a year in California and even less on a national average. Obviously the head of a family who must contend with the U.S. cost of living cannot survive the unfair competition of braceroism. The alternative to a fair wage is relief. Some manage to eke out a living by combining farm work, odd jobs, and county relief. But it is a marginal existence, devoid of dignity and hope for a share in America's future.

Agribusiness contends that a wage hike would not solve the problem because most domestics are unsuited to the rigors of the field and the "stoop labor" required to pick row crops. "Most of our unemployed have work habits which make farm labor unattractive to them," declared Jesse W. Tappe, board chairman of the Bank of America and president of the California Board of Agriculture. Life in the fields *is* arduous. The job may involve stooping, digging, cutting, pulling, climbing, reaching, and lifting. The environment is one of choking dust, searing heat, cold, rain, and mud. Scratches, cuts, and insect bites add to the discomfort.

The supposed fragility of the domestic work force is rather absurd on its face. The bulk of the force is made up of Mexican-Americans, born in Mexico or only a generation or two removed, whose physical endurance matches that of the bracero. And rugged conditions are not the monopoly of agriculture: lumberjacks, fishermen, railroad crews, and other outdoor workers face equally severe conditions. "There's no job that Americans won't do if they get paid for it," asserts C. Al Green, director of the AFL-CIO Agricultural Workers Organizing Committee. "The argument that braceros must be brought into the country because domestics won't do the work is ridiculous. How many braceros do you find working as floor layers, cement masons, roofers? What is worse than working as a roofer, with the hot tar stinking in your face all day, or cleaning out the sewers? But you find Americans doing this work because they get paid well." There are, of course, some conditions that are beyond the endurance of mad dogs, Englishmen—and braceros. In 1962, five hundred braceros quit the melon harvest in California and returned to Mexico, exhausted after working twelve to fourteen hours a day, seven days a week, in hundred-degree-plus weather.

Still the notion of domestic incapability—and resulting shortages—persists. Unlike many other industries which have set up their own recruiting apparatus, most of agribusiness prefers to pass the buck to the state departments of employment. The system in use by the California Department of Employment's Farm Placement Service works like this in the city of Stockton. At 4 A.M. several thousand men mill about the farm labor office in Stockton's Skid Row, shivering in the pre-dawn. About a hundred dilapidated buses parked and double-parked, obstructing the narrow streets. Men continue to emerge from the nearby flophouses in South El Dorado Street. The shape-up is on for domestic agricultural workers. These are not braceros. Some are husbands and fathers. Some are Mexican immigrants, others are Southern white and Negro migrants. Some Filipinos, white Texans, and Oklahomans complete the mob. By four-thirty labor contractors are telling the workers they have selected to start boarding the buses and trucks that will take them to work. All is confusion. Pickets carry protest signs. "It's like a mechanized slave market," says one angry labor organizer. A few hundred men still hang around the Farm Labor Office or the third-rate coffee shops. A few drift toward the still-closed saloons. Some plop down in a vacant lot and take out bottles of cheap wine.

This is the "day haul" system, the daily shape-up which is virtually extinct in other industry. Some of the "domestics" are derelicts and winos interested only in making enough for the next bottle. It is significant that around Stockton, as around similar agricultural hubs, there are thousands of shacks and shanties housing stable family men who consider themselves farm workers at heart.

Most of them, in their humble dignity, refuse to submit
to the shape-up system and the abysmally low wages
offered through the farm labor offices. Many will hire out
through labor contractors who offer slightly higher wages
and the hope of some tenure. But these contractors are
not government-regulated and cheating the worker is
commonplace. Even if he knows he is being cheated, the
worker has no practical redress; if he quits, his "white
card" will be lifted and he will be unable to work until it
is routinely restored.

With a system of this nature, agribusiness can cite incident after incident and impressive statistics to "prove"
the instability of the domestic force. What aggravates the
situation is that state employment officials, although nom-
inally neutral, more often than not are in the growers'
corner. They play ball with the growers because they
move in the same social circles, frequent the same clubs,
attend the same churches, and live next door. This the
domestic worker knows, and he knows the futility of ex-
pecting the local farm labor offices to press his interests.

During the Los Angeles Department of Labor hearings,
farm worker Delmer Berg of Stockton told why most domestics shun the state labor offices: "Most of us resident
workers stay away from the Farm Placement offices. We
know where the jobs are and look for them ourselves. We
know that the Farm Labor offices are engaged in the
business of supplying large growers with cheap labor.
When we get to an office, unless we put up a fight, we are
always referred to the lowest-paying jobs. For instance,
one of my friends is working in carrots and she makes
about three dollars a day. Work is done on a piecerate
basis and formerly a worker picked a fifty-pound sack for

twelve cents. Now a worker must pick a hundred-pound sack for just twelve cents! The reason they can get people to top carrots at this rate is that they must earn enough to buy groceries. Of course it's a violation of state law for a woman to lift a hundred-pound sack, but they have to do it in carrot-topping."

An episode that occurred in Oxnard not long ago demonstrates a case of outright connivance between growers and the state officials. Cesar Chavez, a courageous and dedicated thirty-seven-year-old Mexican-American who publishes the Spanish-language *El Malcriado: Voice of the Farm Worker,* told of his investigation of a "referral system" that at one time was operating in the Oxnard area. While Public Law 78 clearly stipulated that American workers were to be given preference over braceros, Chavez discovered that in Oxnard many local domestics were unable to get jobs. He joined the ranks of these people and found that a worker who applied to the Farm Placement Service office was referred to the local growers' association. There he was dispatched to the carrot fields, where wages were low. The other higher-paying crops were completely dominated by braceros.

For many weeks Chavez met with a group of workers every morning, secured referral cards from the Farm Placement Service, and then applied at the growers' association, only to be turned down cold. The ordinary worker, being powerless, shrugs and accepts defeats of this sort. But Chavez made a habit of filing complaints with the director of the California Farm Placement Service. Over the course of several months he actually filed 1100 complaints. Eventually he telephoned a U. S. Labor Department inspector in Los Angeles and persuaded him to come to Oxnard to inspect a field where braceros were working illegally.

The inspector ordered the grower to remove the braceros and hire local people. The grower complied, but when the inspector returned to Los Angeles the locals were dismissed and the braceros put back to work! This scene was repeated again and again until the day Cesar Chavez led over a hundred workers to a field after notifying newspapers and television stations of his intent.

The publicity that was stirred up triggered a thorough probe of the Farm Placement Service. One assistant chief was fired for accepting bribes from growers. Edward F. Hayes and two other employees resigned, and an unknown number of employees received letters of "censure and reprimand." *Not long afterward Edward Hayes became the manager of the Imperial Valley Farmers' Association.*

The discouragement of being ousted by braceros, the miserable conditions in the fields, the lack of a wage floor, and the hostility of employers have driven many domestic workers to cover. Where are they? Many still live in agricultural areas, in pathetic hovels, foraging for a subsistence. In Tracy, California, the mother of a permanent farm worker family of six, living in a condemned shack, reflected the mood of desperation: "We didn't have enough work in the fields this year, so I don't know what we'll do if they finally tear this place down . . . and I don't think the growers or unions or anyone else will ever change things for us." Others are better off idle and drawing relief checks than sweating for the token wages of the field. Many more have gravitated to the cities, finding sporadic work in the manufacturing industries.

A 1964 study of the metropolitan Los Angeles unemployment picture revealed the extent of the untapped urban pool. The study was conducted by researchers attached to the University of California at Los Angeles Institute of Industrial Relations. It was found that one half of the thousands interviewed in areas of heavy unemployment were originally from farms and small towns. Thirty-one per cent of the males said they could be attracted back to the farms if basic standards of decency and pay were introduced. Such responses might ordinarily be viewed with skepticism, but in early 1965 the State Department of Employment *did* place 34 per cent of those approached to do farm work.

The UCLA study was incorporated into a report entitled *After the Bracero*. It was written by Fred H. Schmidt, a native of the Texas cotton region who had previously been an aide to Congressman Henry Gonzales of San Antonio. Schmidt proceeded on the premise that agribusiness is going to have to face up to the reality of cultivating its own labor force. "So long as there is any assurance that a reservoir of foreign labor can readily be tapped to meet what appear to be shortages of labor supply," reasoned Schmidt, "there will be continuing postponements in reckoning with the basic problems associated with farm labor." He stressed that the present concept of "casualization" of the work force is outmoded, and that the denial of unemployment benefits to farm workers must end if a permanent force is to be mobilized.

The "casual" concept is part of the legend that domestics are almost to a man rootless and migratory, faceless men whom a grower will never see again. According to the U. S. Departments of Labor and Agriculture, however, *domestic migrants number only 228,000 of the 8.3 million persons employed in farm work in September, the peak month.* Other sources raise the number into the low millions. Whatever the count, migrants are only a fraction of the force. And they are not nomads by choice. No man looks forward to piling his family into a rattle-trap car or patched-up old school bus and limping from one hostile community to another, seeking a grassy field or ditch bank to sleep on and hoping a friendly filling station will let his wife and children use the rest room. Every man instinctively desires identification; he aspires to have a place he can call home, the chance to become part of a community, the opportunity to put his children in school.

The prospect that an end to braceroism will disrupt the traditional pattern of migration is a live fear with agribusiness. In its September 1964 issue, the *Del Monte Shield,* house organ of the California Packing Corporation, expressed it this way: "It is expected that the citrus farmer who successfully replaces braceros with domestic Mexican-Americans may well deprive the apple grower in Washington, the sugar beet grower in Idaho, or the cucumber grower in Michigan of his labor supply; the tomato grower in New Jersey or in eastern Pennsylvania may find the Puerto Rican labor that he depended upon for so many years has been recruited by a peach farmer in Arkansas or a cotton grower in Texas."

The implication of this thesis is that the bracero, as the hard core of the labor force, has put the domestic on the move scouring the country for the lean pickings. What the passage describes, actually, is *a free labor market* in which growers must vie for workers with inducements such as higher pay and better conditions. This is anathema to agribusiness. The *Shield* article clings to the idea that "America always has been and still is dependent on imported labor to harvest its food and fiber crops." In this rich tradition, the *Shield* blandly notes, "*our earliest commercial farmers imported African Negroes as slaves to work the cotton and tobacco fields.*" Evidently it sees little virtue in kicking this grand old habit.

California Packing is not unique in resisting change in the status quo. In fact, the company's "enlightened self-interest," as one of its executives phrased it, is more progressive than most and Cal-Pak deserves credit for the steps it has taken in the right direction. In reporting on the labor situation in its divisions last year, the company stated: "Before 1959, the California Division used braceros extensively. But four years ago, seeing that for its operations *the disadvantages of the bracero program outweighed the advantages,* the Division began an active domestic recruitment program. Today, its farm labor force is made up of Americans of Mexican descent from Texas and the Southwest, who supplement local workers, and migrant families who return to Cal-Pak ranches each year. In 1963, only about fifty braceros were used. They were hired for a very short period to complete the fig harvest. *The Division's effort to replace braceros has had marked success, probably because the Division sets high standards in feeding, housing, and wages.* In addition, the Division keeps in touch with former workers at intervals and encourages them to return to the California Division, and at the end of the season distributes 'merit cards' which identify the holder as a good worker and give him first opportunity at employment the following season." (Italics added.)

The replaceability of the bracero has been discovered by other growers who have made an attempt to develop an attached domestic force. A prominent Florida grower declares: "I've never had a labor problem. Maybe that's because labor comes first here. I try and put up a good product but not at the expense of the poverty, misery, and suffering of my workers."

Bud Antle, an Arizona-based grower who styles himself "Lettuce King of the World," takes the positive approach. "Give me a market and I'll get the lettuce" is the sort of remark that has drawn frowns from fellow growers. But Antle, who started as a lettuce trimmer in 1931 and now ships 10,000 carloads a year, has looked beyond the bracero for some time. "It's easier to complain than to get the job done," he remarks. Antle attracts all the help he needs with higher wages and amenities such as air-conditioned buses to transport workers from town. Last year Antle bused his crews home to California for the Easter holiday.

There will be enough workers and no spoiled crops when growers face up to their responsibility to fill their labor needs in a competitive market, and recognize need for dramatic improvements in the salaries and working conditions of our country's most deprived workers.

8 ARMAGEDDON FOR AGRIBUSINESS

I

Armageddon for agribusiness was December 31, 1964. On that day Public Law 78, the bracero law, finally expired without renewal by Congress. The year before, one member of Congress after another had entered the well of the House and made it plain that patience with braceroism was exhausted, that agribusiness must solve its own labor problems within the confines of typical American free enterprise. The late Edward R. Murrow had called the plight of the domestic worker America's "Harvest of Shame"; the Senate subcommittee on migratory labor had called it "a national disgrace." John Steinbeck in his 1936 *The Grapes of Wrath* had written: "There is a crime here that goes beyond denunciation. There is a sorrow here that weeping cannot symbolize. There is a failure here that

topples all our success." Steinbeck observed that in three
decades nothing had changed. As everyone knew, the ma-
trix of the problem was cheap foreign labor. But agribusiness was not going to release its grip without a struggle.
The Santa Clara County, California, Democratic Council
prophesied: "The transition from an exploitative attitude,
whose overriding consideration was profit, to an attitude
whose primary concern is to fully involve the farm laborer in the affluence of this society will be painful."

The prediction was understated. Singly and as a group,
from Florida to California, agricultural interests continued to oppose the clear will of the American people as
expressed by Congress. The last-ditch battle was aimed
at wooing the public on the one hand, and winning
renewed political support on the other. All the old chest-
nuts trumping up the bracero were dragged out, and
some new ones added. The agribusiness lobby button-
holded members of Congress to keep the bracero program
alive—in one form or another.

The gnashing of teeth lent the impression that Congress
had been heedless to the growers' arguments, that it had
made a rash and arbitrary decision. Such was not the
case. The Department of Labor had for years held hearings on the subject, listening to the grower and labor
side alike. In a statement at the end of Public Law 78,
Secretary of Labor Willard Wirtz found it high time that
"the miserable working conditions maintained by some
of the growers be ended." In the face of growing complaints against the importation of underpaid foreign labor
Wirtz praised the Eighty-eighth Congress for outlawing
braceroism and recognizing the need to provide decent
conditions for American farm labor. "The Eighty-eighth

Congress was a humanitarian Congress. It passed the Civil Rights Act, ending a century of racial discrimination. It passed the Anti-Poverty bill, declaring war on mankind's oldest enemy. Quietly, with little public attention at the time, it also decided to stop the 'Mexican bracero program,' ending fourteen years of a system that had too often disregarded human values."

Despite ample warning that its supplies of foreign labor were to be cut off, agribusiness did little but clamor for extensions of Public Law 78. Wirtz remained adamant. "The various proposals to extend Public Law 78 by administrative action of one kind or another fly squarely in the face of the decision made by Congress," he replied. "These proposals must be, and they are, rejected."

Yet Wirtz bent over backward to accommodate agribusiness, placing himself in a position that started what might be called "back-door braceroism." The McCarran-Walter Immigration Act, Public Law 414, stipulates that aliens can be admitted for temporary service or labor if "capable" domestics are not available. The late Senator Pat McCarran had pushed this bill through in the early fifties to assure his Nevada ranch cronies a steady stream of Basque sheepherders. The catchword is "capable." No Americans are capable of putting on the incomparable —to some incomprehensible—exhibitions of the Beatles, so the British performers are admitted under Public Law 414. Wirtz agreed to let agribusiness bring in the lowly bracero so it could be absolutely demonstrated that sufficient capable Americans were unavailable.

Foes of braceroism saw in this a ploy to bring about a de facto braceroism that might linger long enough to

become a new status quo. Indeed the Jesuit Father James
L. Vizzard thought the proposal resisted the intent of
Congress' decision. He told a Department of Labor hearing on the matter that he had "no tears to waste on
those who have been crying disaster at the prospect of
losing the previously available agricultural workers from
Mexico under Public Law 78 but who in the meantime
have taken no realistic steps to secure an adequate and
dependable U.S. labor force." He could not help but
condemn "those who, if we let them, will create or exploit
new devices, such as loopholes in Public Law 414, to
secure docile, underpaid alien workers." He deplored
"those politicians who feel they must cooperate with the
growers in their continued refusal to face the demands
of individual justice and the common good. . . . Since
these growers show no signs of self-reform, they need
to be told emphatically and with finality that the approximation of slave-labor conditions which they have per-
petuated will no longer be tolerated by this nation. They
need to be made to understand in what century and in
what kind of country and in what kind of economy and
society they are living and operating. They must be forced
to realize that to exploit the poverty of other nations in
order to beat down and crush the poor of our own country
is the grossest kind of immorality."

But the good Father's ringing rebuttal failed to carry
the day. When the final sordid chapter of braceroism in
the United States is written, it will be recorded that
Secretary Wirtz gave agribusiness, in his desire to be
fair, every benefit of the doubt. That risk was a great one,
because as he himself said, "The stakes here are high:

tens of thousands of jobs for otherwise unemployed men and women; the survival of a great many business enterprises; the winning of a fight for human decency."

II

An orderly transition seemed precisely what agribusiness did not want, for it stubbornly adhered to the proposition that there could be no order without the bracero. In the early months of 1965, as the first of the harvests neared, the combined forces of agribusiness interests launched a full-scale offensive to carry the point to the public. The strategy considered that if the public could be swayed, Congress would follow suit.

California took the brunt of the campaign, since it supplies some 40 per cent of the nation's food and generates $3.6 billion a year in agricultural receipts. California was also the state that leaned most decisively on the bracero: in 1963 it employed 110,823 as compared with 26,084 for Texas and 15,857 for Arizona.

Since the American conscience rebels at the thought of preventable waste, a most effective technique was to raise the chimera of crops rotting in the fields due to a lack of labor. Conservative U. S. Senator George Murphy —dutifully repeating the message of the large growers— warned that losses would run into the millions; illogically, the scapegoat in Murphy's book was not Congress but Secretary Wirtz for not allowing braceros to pour in fast enough under the McCarran-Walter Act. Wirtz, alleged Murphy, was inflicting a "catastrophe" on both farmers and food buyers by his "incredibly stubborn refusal to permit farmers to have necessary supplemental harvest labor from Mexico."

To dramatize his point, ex-actor Murphy flew to California and appeared at the farm of Orange County strawberry grower Jack Tabata. As television cameras recorded the scene, Tabata plowed under a single row of berries while Murphy glowered with indignation. "Every day they wait to bring back braceros adds to the tragedy here," he cried. Then he danced north to stage a similar performance in the Salinas Valley, the "Lettuce Capital of the World."

The refrain was picked up by other grower protagonists. California Employment director Albert Tieburg, an affable man caught in the crossfire, said that Wirtz "has to be convinced that he's doing great economic harm." This was echoed by a spokesman for the powerful Council of California Growers, who held Wirtz personally responsible for "a shortage of farm workers" that will cause "tremendous losses" in Salinas Valley strawberry crops and probably in forthcoming harvests. "Contrary to Secretary of Labor Wirtz's statements that he would not allow crops to rot, crops are rotting due to a labor shortage," said the spokesman. The Bank of America joined in the arm-twisting by raising the specter of paralyzed farm economy: it announced it was suspending financing of growers "unless there was some assurance of labor supplies."

The "shortage" hue and cry spilled over on Governor Edmund "Pat" Brown. Two ultraconservatives in the State Senate, Jack Schrade of San Diego and John G. Schmitz of Santa Ana, a member of the John Birch Society, announced they would start recall proceedings.

The move was based on a speech on the floor of the U. S. House of Representatives by Republican James B. Utt, another ultraconservative Bircher from the prosperous citrus-growing area of Orange County, blaming Brown and Secretary Wirtz for "a man-made catastrophe" because of limitations on the number of Mexicans admitted. In his hyperbolic speech, Utt had said: "I have requested the President to declare farm areas of California relief areas and provide immediate relief to farmers' allied industries, which are damaged because of the failure to harvest our crops."

The attack on Governor Brown was heavy with irony. A man of humane instincts, Brown had insisted, when he first took office in 1959, that the farm laborer be included in the minimum wage coverage. "If a person is worth hiring," he had said, "he is worth paying a decent living wage. The special interest group which denies that, imperils its own future as well as California's." Yet as time went on, Brown became caught in a slowly-turning vise. When debate on the termination of Public Law 78 raged, he came out in favor of a gradual phase-out over an additional five years. When the "rotting crops" crisis arose, he issued a plea to Wirtz to ease the "desperate" farm labor situation by authorizing more braceros.

The position of the growers was underscored when planeloads of Guamanians and Puerto Ricans, technically not imported labor, arrived in California. The makeshift approach of the Department of Employment, which recruited college students, housewives, persons on relief, Sioux Indians, and drifters, and even arranged for the early parole of prisoners on the proviso they work in the fields, heightened the image of a stricken industry.

Yet *where the semblance of a decent wage and steady work was offered, domestic workers responded with enthusiasm.* A Ventura County lemon grower reported: "The first ones they [the Department of Employment] sent us were dregs, but now the growers are paying higher and getting good men." In Blythe, melon growers who offered $1.75 an hour plus a twenty-five-cents-an-hour bonus for staying to the end of the harvest were swamped with delighted workers.

An experiment conducted by the Interfaith Migrant Committee called the bluff of Salinas Valley strawberry growers who were crying wolf the loudest. Wirtz had pegged $1.40 an hour as the rate which had to be offered domestic workers before quotas of braceros would be considered. This amounted to *$56 for a forty-hour week*, not much in a state where the average weekly wage in manufacturing is more than $120 and still below the $1.62½ an hour that had prevailed before the bracero flood crested in 1954. But it was a marked improvement over the approximate $1 an hour in effect the year before.

Convinced there was a sizable group of disaffected farm workers in the shantytowns clustered around Gilroy and San Jose, the Committee organized a door-to-door recruitment effort. Buses filled for the three-hour round trip to the Salinas farms. Within a month, giant Salinas Strawberries, Inc., announced it was sending home its allotment of braceros as soon as contract guarantees were met; it would not exercise an option to employ 1900 braceros for an additional sixty days.

The dire predictions of crop loss proved wrong. Where losses did occur, they were due, in virtually every instance, to poor planning, nature—or deliberate artifice. Some growers had continued to assume that the government would grant them an unlimited supply of cheap labor and had overplanted on speculation. The 1965 growing season was marked by capricious weather, which took its toll. Some advertised plow-unders were nothing more than routine destruction of worn-out plants in accordance with proper scientific practice. A San Joaquin asparagus grower who claimed to have plowed under seventy-five acres because of a shortage of help was tartly told by Director of Employment Tieburg: "We could have supplied any number of qualified workers."

The proof of the pudding was in the eating: Golden State crops flowed to the nation's tables, and the state held its position as the leading agricultural producer for the eighteenth consecutive year. Over all, said Tieburg, California farming "stands as strong and sound today as it has ever been."

Despite the scary prognostication of Senator Murphy of a five hundred-million-dollar loss, estimated cash receipts from agricultural sales in 1965 moved *about one billion dollars above second-ranked Iowa.* Practically everywhere cheerful notes were struck. Salinas Valley lettuce growers harvested *double* the crop of the year before when they were heavily dependent on braceros, and reaped firm prices. San Joaquin asparagus growers netted a million dollars *more* than the year before, despite paying higher wages. Tomato production ran close to the record year of 1964. A spokesman for the California Tomato Growers Association said his members will never again ask for braceros, admitting "we had a pretty fair year despite our screaming." Glenn E. Brockway, San Francisco chief of the Labor Department, stated that the experience clearly showed that *California could harvest all its crops without foreign labor.*

9 THE TIMELESS SOUTHWEST

It has been difficult for residents of the Southwest to instigate reform measures. In part this is true because unlike other parts of the country where the average citizen is exposed to many different viewpoints, the Southwest is exposed to a decidedly one-sided press. Of course, the press is no more than a reflection of the almost monopolistic rule of the power elite, which often choses to sweep serious social problems under the rug or give them inadequate attention when circumstances are overwhelmingly in favor of the well-to-do, and frequently ignores minority groups and the poor in general.

Take, for example, the Freedom Newspapers chain based in metropolitan Orange County, which boasts the second-highest median family income in the wealthy state of California. The publisher is Raymond C. Hoiles, a Bible-quoting septuagenarian, who carries the doctrine of laissez-faire capitalism to such an extreme that he actually advocates turning over fire and police departments to private enterprise. His columnists sound much like Arizona pundit George Boardman, who condemns Medicare as "socialized medicine" and counsels doctors to "refuse . . . any part of the loot with impunity."

In a debate in the spring of 1964, publisher Hoiles repeated this theme that public schools are nothing more than compulsory indoctrination, and that parents should enroll their children in a private school of their choice. Asked what might happen to the children of parents who were unable to place them in private schools, Hoiles snapped, "Repeal the crazy laws that keep the children from going to work. There'll be plenty of jobs if you keep the government out of it."

Another stumbling block lies in the very nature of poverty. As Dr. Paul O'Rourke has observed, while it is comparatively easy to arouse instinctive public support for campaigns against "killer" diseases like polio, heart disease, and cancer because people fear the diseases themselves or wish to be thought charitable, or seek tax deductions, it is difficult to get people to help the poor whose plight is somehow blamed never on economic injustice but on personal failure.

The most vocal attitude of the ruling classes of the Southwest—but not, I feel strongly, the ingrained opinion of the majority of the people of that region—is pithily stated in the philosophy of former Senator Goldwater of Arizona, who consistently voted against bills designed to help the poor. In a speech in January, 1964, he was explicit: "I do not believe that the mere fact of having little money entitles everybody, regardless of circumstances, to be permanently maintained by the taxpayers at an average or comfortable standard of living."

Goldwater deleted from the same speech a passage which evidently was considered too politically explosive. To wit, the idea that poverty and unemployment were caused by lack of education "was like saying that people have big feet because they wear big shoes. The fact is that most people who have no skill have no education for the same reason—low intelligence or low ambition."

There is little doubt that America's forty million poor would have been largely ignored by a Goldwater in the White House. The former Senator looked skeptically on commonly accepted statistics on poverty in the United States and argued that income levels considered low in this country "are regarded as true wealth in the rest of the world." What he neglected to say was that a man making the equivalent of $1500 a year in, say, Ghana or Peru is truly wealthy. But to the destitute people of Harlem, West Virginia, or the California migrant camps he was saying in effect: "You may think you are terribly poor, but there are people living in villages in Africa and India who would be glad to live in your rat-infested rooms and wear your ragged clothes."

No wonder that *Newsweek* magazine characterized the Goldwater remarks as sounding "more like an all-out attack on the nation's poverty-stricken" than an attack on poverty.

Though he was emphatically denied our nation's highest office, Goldwater did represent Arizona in the nation's capitol for a number of years. There he mirrored the Southwest character, the rugged, blunt-spoken frontier attitude that trusts chiefly the land and the animals. Quite in character, he plugged for the retention of the bracero program that gave big growers cheap manpower at the expense of the domestic farmhand. Quite in character, too, are the unfortunate side effects of Arizona's bluff individualism: the state has one of the highest infant mortality rates in the nation; it has one of the highest rates of young people not in school; it has hundreds of thousands of Mexican-Americans, Indians, and Negroes trapped at the bottom of a caste system. Arizona is a land of extremes: it has more wealthy people per capita than any other state, but also more families who live on $1000 a year or less, an income which figures out to about seventy cents a day per person for food, rent, clothing, medical care, and other expenses.

Though Goldwater himself was apparently poorly informed concerning welfare, there are those in his state who are well versed. In 1961, Howard Gessop, director of the Maricopa County Welfare Department (Phoenix), conducted a wise experiment. He divided four hundred welfare cases into two groups, assigning half to regular social workers with usual heavy caseloads of from two hundred to four hundred each, and half to a special class of social workers who had had at least one year of graduate training and who for the test period carried only forty cases each. After only five months, 23 per cent of the cases assigned to the latter group were off welfare, their medical problems taken care of and their schooling resumed or their job problems solved. The net saving to Goldwater's home county was $5700 per month—a lesson in the investment maxim that it takes money to save money.

At the Tuscon conference, Mrs. Barbara Norton of Scottsdale, Arizona, took issue with those who devote most of their social energies to seeking out "welfare chiselers." Noting that in only 1.9 per cent of the cases in Phoenix was there any evidence of intent to defraud, she urged Arizona welfare administrators to stop being conscientious objectors in the war on poverty and bend their major efforts toward rehabilitating the poor and reducing their dependency.

Now, as a son of the Southwest I await the day it will stir from its lethargy and give *all* of its citizens a place in its glorious sunlight. It may, of course, have to revise some of the quaint old customs such as are still in style in the lovely California town of Santa Barbara. At Fiesta time, Spanish-speaking Americans, no matter what their status, are invited to make themselves at home in the heart of the city, because they lend a certain antique color associated with the area. But when Fiesta is over, they are no longer welcome. They melt away and once again become invisible, facing the hard life in the best way they can.

10 AFTER THE BRACERO, WHAT?

I

One of the most frequent complaints of growers is that "do-gooders" and "bleeding hearts" have meddled in something beyond their economic comprehension. "It is all very well to dabble in social causes," they say, "but those who press the issue too far just don't understand the pragmatics of the situation." If the 1965 tug of war in California did nothing else, it afforded the gentlemen growers a refresher course in the free-enterprise doctrine that is their political creed.

San Joaquin asparagus growers, for example, netted a million dollars *more* than in the previous year even though paying higher wages, an accomplishment forced upon them because they had to abide by the basic precept of supply and demand. They had to plan their output carefully to match anticipated demand, and throw away the dice with which they had formerly gambled on over-plant at the expense of the worker. Prices held firm and profit margins steadied.

As the government withdrew from the role of labor procurer, the free marketplace assumed command. When the din was the loudest during the 1965 harvest, Secretary Wirtz flew to California to see with his own eyes what the actual situation was. Refusing to be led by the nose, he trudged unannounced from field to field, seeing condi-tions in the raw. One of his first reactions was repugnance at finding no field toilets on the farms he visited. He was repelled by the filthy conditions at one of the largest labor camps in the state, but complimented a large grower who maintained neat and clean barracks.

It was evident to Wirtz that growers were reaping what they had sown in terms of treatment of workers. "The most serious reports of labor turnover," he observed, "came from farm operations where conditions were bad, and the fewest complaints from places that obviously were well operated. Where growers have good work camps, most workers stay on the job. Those with bad work camps find their workers leaving them."

Growers who had groused about high taxes could note with pleasure the lifting of tax drains. Curtailment of the bracero system saves the government tens of millions of dollars annually in administrative costs; taxpayers no longer must subsidize a multibillion dollar industry by underwriting procurement costs. *The reduced numbers of braceros in California in 1965 had a dramatic effect, too, on welfare costs. Twenty thousand more Americans were on the job.* Spotlighting the Salinas Valley, 313 families had been on the welfare rolls as of April, 1964, when the bracero was still the mainstay of the work force; by April, 1965 the number had dropped to seventy-seven families because of new job openings on the farm. In other agricultural areas of the state the pattern was the same.

Economists have detected a healthy effect on the prosperity of farm communities. *Braceros took back to Mexico with them an estimated thirty million dollars each year, spending only a trickle in the United States. Now the money is being plowed back into local communities by American workers.* And with the artificial depressant of braceroism gone wages are creeping up to the point where workers will in the not too distant future be able to buy homes, appliances, and automobiles. Ironically, too, they will be able to afford the crops they harvested—tomatoes, fruit, and lettuce—whereas before they subsisted largely on a diet of starches.

This is not to say the 25 per cent to 50 per cent wage boost in some areas adds up to what the average laboring man would call a good salary; it is merely that the old scale was so deplorably low that the new wages look generous by comparison. The end of braceroism—if it is really the end—has concomitantly given new life to the small farmer, who formerly was up against unfair competition every time he climbed on his tractor, having to pit his own time against that of a low-wage bracero driving an agribusiness tractor. Low wage scales and bad conditions of employment hurt not just the laborer but the independent farmer as well, especially the good man who is trying to treat his workers and their families like human beings.

A resurgence of independent farming when wages sub-

Labor, the Land,
and the
Struggle for Justice

stantially appreciate could follow because eliminating cheap labor could break corporation monopoly control of California fruits and vegetables, a stranglehold that has been killing off the individualist farmer. Many independent growers large and small have been led to believe that the bracero program is in their best interests. It is not.

An optimistic prognosis was advanced by Governor Brown in testimony before a House labor subcommittee considering legislation that would bring farm workers under federal minimum wage laws for the first time (the minimum would start at $1.15 an hour and graduate over two years to $1.25, the present minimum for industrial workers). Brown said the end of the bracero program promised to be a boon to growers and farm workers alike.

"Employment is up," he noted. "Wages are up. Production is high and farm prices are generally stable." Agriculture is undergoing revolutionary changes, he pointed out, with everything pointing to increased efficiency and profits for growers. "Certainly labor should be allowed to share in those benefits," remarked Brown. Scoffing at grower excuses that they cannot afford wage hikes, he charged: "This is exactly the same argument garment manufacturers made years ago in trying to preserve the miserable sweatshops where women and children slaved under inhuman conditions for a pittance." He urged Congress not to be misled by some of the complaints it is hearing about the California farm situation. "Paid professional propagandists have twisted the facts out of shape," he said.

II

The warning of agribusiness spokesmen that wage increases would mean sharp increases in supermarket prices is a plea for sympathy from the American housewife. Senator Murphy, for one, has depicted soaring food prices; the Council of California Growers has hinted broadly that he is right. The facts, however, draw a different picture.

The cost of field labor is two to five cents on the dollar, depending on the crop. Even a substantial wage raise— as much as double—would hardly be noticed by the housewife. Decent farm wages would add less than half a cent to the price of a head of lettuce, for example. Grocery-store prices in the store are not a true reflection of wages in the field. As Secretary Wirtz put it after his California tour, "There can be no Americans who would find a fraction-of-a-penny increase in the price of, say, a can of tomatoes or a dozen oranges too high to alleviate some of the conditions of poverty we saw on our tour."

All of this is assuming that the cost of field labor is transmitted directly to the housewife. There is a broad cushion between the field and the supermarket shelf that could easily absorb the raise in whole or in part without cutting into profits. Labor leader C. Al Green gives an illustration: "Take a No. 2½ can of tomatoes, containing approximately two pounds of tomatoes, and selling for twenty-five cents. If the farmer is getting twenty-five dollars per ton for his tomatoes, he is getting 1.25 cents per pound. His share of that can of tomatoes is 2.5 cents.

The remaining 22.5 cents goes to the processor, shipper, wholesaler, and retailer. The tomato *picker* gets considerably less than one cent."

A bit of quick arithmetic shows that if the housewife's price of the can of tomatoes was raised one cent, and the whole cent went to the farmer, he could raise the wages of his workers 50 per cent and still make five dollars more per ton. The cent could be nicely assimilated along the lengthy route from field to market.

That the housewife should lay the blame for rising food prices elsewhere than at the doorstep of the small farm and fieldworker is a premise of the National Commission on Food Marketing, which is prying into what happens after food leaves the fields. Stock splits and black-ink financial reports attest to the healthy conditions of the big middlemen. Performance records of integrated producers like California Packing and Stokely-Van Camp show earnings at a steady pace. *Di Giorgio Fruit announced a 10 per cent jump in earnings for the quarter ended September 30, 1965, a period covering the bracero "crisis."*

J. Earl Coke, agricultural economist and former vice president of the Bank of America, predicted a rosy future for agribusiness in the course of a 1963 address: "With national population expected to reach or exceed three hundred million in the next twenty-five years, and with per capita consumer income expected to continue its upward climb, the total demand for food can only increase —even in the absence of any new international markets. Probably as significant as the changes in total demand will be the changes that occur in people's tastes as we become more affluent. New dietary fads and new health discoveries are impossible to predict, of course. But the trend toward more beef, more citrus and fruits, and more green leafy vegetables appears likely to continue. If so, prices should remain strong for many of the farm products which California and the Southwest are equipped, climatically, to produce."

The variety of crops for which Coke anticipates rising demand is least adaptable to mechanization. The huge threshers and combines that move like juggernauts through Midwestern grainfields have pared the need for farm labor there. But even though a degree of mechanization is coming to the crops of the West and Southwest, the long-range requirements for labor will remain up.

In his speech Coke also commented: "We have seen California agriculture advance from an agrarian economy to the domain of science, engineering, and business management." Surely agribusiness, if it had the will, could put this modern capability to work solving its labor problems. By means of an electronic communications hookup and a computerized nerve center it could manage its labor force with cost-saving efficiency. Research aimed at creating crop strains which would ripen at present slack periods would help flatten the demand for workers. Strategic relocation of various crops to create a harvest cycle within a limited area would cut down on travel time for workers and enable them to live permanently in the hub of the area. An approximation of this condition actually exists, according to one labor leader, in the Stockton, California, area. With proper planning, he insists, a labor force could remain busy nine months of the year within a fifty-mile radius of

Stockton. Concentration will have to focus, too, on *family* housing, since many of the replacements for the single bracero will be family men.

III

In the summer of 1965 the root of the housing problem was graphically shown in Visalia, in the fertile Central Valley of California. Two hundred and twenty families working the melon and tomato harvests were crammed into eleven-by-sixteen shanties built in 1938 by the federal government as a stopgap emergency housing facility. The shacks have no glass windows, front doors, or plumbing. The "fruit tramps," as they are often contemptuously referred to, protested when rents for these hovels were raised to twenty-five dollars a month. The rural slum was operated by Tulare County, whose housing manager conceded: "My personal opinion is that nobody in this day and age should have to live in these things."

On the market today are many designs of inexpensive prefabricated and portable housing that could be easily adapted to solve the problems of the fields. There are three distinct types of housing problems, according to the time the shelter is needed: permanent, intermediate, and what is called "flash peak." The latter is the most urgent; it is needed for those short harvest seasons during which families now live on ditch banks and under bridges. As a matter of fact, Sam Van der Ryn, professor of environmental design at the University of California, designed a substitute for permanent-type housing for flash peaks that would not be too prohibitive for farmers or private speculators. Its feasibility was demonstrated on Friday, May 28, 1965, when—with impoverished families living like animals without water or toilets in the weeds along the banks of Mormon Slough and a nearby sun-dried field—anti-poverty money was at last released to the San Joaquin Community Action Council. Just seven days later on June 4, an encampment of cheerful yellow-and-white and blue-and-white prefab houses mushroomed up in the field around a trio of easily removable buildings that housed showers, washing machines, a child-care nursery, and a clinic. Nearby was a 320-foot deep well; from its plastic pipe bubbled clear running water to the village. Electricity was turned on. Clean portable toilets dotted the streets. The relieved families began to move in off the ditch bank late in the day. The air was festive. The colorful twelve-sided, dome-roofed houses, with alternating panels of fiberglass and screen supported by aluminum frames, took weary American families out of *The Grapes of Wrath* and into the 1960s in just a few hours.

The portable village, *with each house costing only $240 complete,* can be folded like an accordian and carted to the next flash-peak area. As revealing as the demonstration was, there were conservative skeptics who opposed it at every turn. Until rancher Kaufmann agreed to rent his land, one prospective site after another was taken off the market. "There were the die-hards," reported the *Chronicle,* "still fighting for the bracero as ideal stoop labor."

Frederick R. Blackwell, chief counsel for the Senate subcommittee on migratory labor, pleaded with growers to use "the genius that brought your agricultural production to the pinnacle of the world to bring agricultural labor up to that pinnacle." It was evident that if half the time, work, thought, private money, and tax money that had gone into the bracero program were diverted to building a domestic labor force, braceroism would soon become a dim, easily forgotten chapter in the history of American agriculture.

But it was not to be. Although the Council of California Growers admitted that the "days of large-scale importation of foreign workers are over," and other grower groups faced up to the responsibility of working with American labor, an influential segment of agribusiness remained intransigent. Senator Murphy, speaking to a convention of Arizona and California growers in San Francisco in November, 1965, said growers had suffered heavily from government "mismanagement" of farm labor problems, and that they would continue to suffer if they did not fight "encroachment by big government." G. Stewart Boswell of the National Council of Agricultural Employers told the powerful Western Growers Association, which had not abandoned the fight for braceros, that it must "redouble its efforts." In May, 1965, the ultraconservative United Republicans of California actually passed a resolution to promote restoration of braceroism!

The National Council of Agricultural Employers was set up by agribusiness in May, 1964, when it became apparent that Congress meant what it said about shutting off the bracero flow. The Council operates on the political and propaganda fronts, as a jointly supported vehicle of agribusiness interests. In 1965 California Packing Employment and Labor Relations Manager G. C. Henry, whose company supports the Council, commented: "Foreign labor involves our immigration laws . . . and all of us must be prepared to spend a lot of time on this problem in Washington, D.C." That the effort is directed at a return to full-scale braceroism is indicated by what Henry saw in his crystal ball: "In the long run we will continue to use supplemental foreign agricultural labor and will adopt government programs to do this."

It is beyond doubt that it is just to
seek aid if the employers place unjust
burdens upon the workers, or degrade them
with conditions which are repugnant to
their dignity as human beings.

—POPE LEO XIII

II DELANO

I

On February 4, 1966, I drove north out of Los Angeles,
headed for the vineyards of Delano, where since September 8, 1965, farm workers have waged one of the most
important strikes in the history of the American labor
movement. Though I had followed reports of the controversy for months, carefully studying the arguments of
both sides, I wanted now to visit the theater of operations
myself.

I knew that in the Delano area Mexican-Americans,
Filipinos, Puerto Ricans, Negroes, and Anglos were working together in an effort to achieve a victory that the
rest of American labor had won over thirty years ago.

Having read a great deal of literature published by
the growers, I was struck by the remarkable similarity

between what they were saying now and what other shortsighted representatives of management and capital had said so many years earlier. In 1900, George Baer, president of the Reading Coal and Iron Company, commented on the anthracite strike then being waged: "The rights and interests of the laboring man will be protected and cared for . . . not by the labor agitators, but by the Christian men to whom God in His infinite wisdom has given the control of the property interests of this country."

Now, in 1966, Joseph Brosmer, spokesman for the growers' Agricultural Labor Bureau was saying: "Those pickers don't want a union, they've got a real fine relationship with the employers . . . really personal. A union would destroy it."

Six and a half decades apart, these statements of benevolent paternalism were uttered by management spokesmen whose industries were threatened with what they saw as the ultimate bête noire: unionism. During that long interval, collective bargaining has come to every major American industry with the exception of agribusiness. It had to be introduced because of the wide gap between management's concept of the "rights and interests of the laboring man" and the laboring man's own concept. At Delano, the main issues were rights of collective bargaining and wages. Joseph Brosmer had shrugged off the issue with the statement "A good examination proves the wage rate is adequate."

To whom? The "adequate" rate before the strike, in many fields, was $1.25 an hour. Strikers thought it should be raised to $1.40 an hour, the *minimum* set by Secretary Wirtz during the 1965 "crisis," that had to be offered to

Americans before the bracero could be considered. Since the proposed minimum wage for nonagricultural workers in California is $2 an hour, the demand did not seem extravagant.

Since the reader may think of his own salary in weekly rather than hourly terms it is instructive to consider that a man making even $2 an hour will earn only $80 for a forty-hour week. With deductions his check will come to less than $70, not exactly a princely sum on which to raise a family.

Behind the specific issues of the Delano strike looms the ancient callousness of agribusiness nationally toward its workers. Because the worker-poor are looked upon merely as a commodity—along with electric power, irrigation water, and farm machinery—they are treated as a commodity. It would be absurd to ship cattle or cotton or grain in buses; therefore it seems pointless to many growers to bother about even minimum standards of comfort and safety in the transportation of farm workers. If the worker is relatively fortunate he may ride in a bus, although it will probably be a vehicle so dilapidated that one wonders how it continues to run. Normally he will be hauled about in trucks. No one—except the passengers—will give much thought to the fact that the truck probably will have worn brakes, bald tires, inadequate lights, and other mechanical faults. Nor will executives lose sleep over the overcrowding that is common in farm transportation.

During the long years of discomfort, accidents, and misery the federal government never required crew leaders to carry as much as liability insurance on farm workers while they were being transported. In 1965 the long-overdue requirement was established. Among the impelling reasons were three tragic accidents that occured in 1963. In Florida a truck loaded with migrants hooked bumpers with a bus and plunged into a canal. Twenty-seven were drowned, including twelve children who should have been in school. Not long after that a busload of sixty-three Mexican workers returning from the celery fields near Chualar, California, was hit by a Southern Pacific freight train at a secondary crossing. A lettuce worker in a nearby field reported, "Bodies just flew all over the place." The death toll was thirty-two. A few days later in Westmoreland, California, in the Imperial Valley, another busload of farm workers spun off the road into a drainage canal. Thirty-nine were injured, four seriously.

If any further justification is needed to give the farm worker a collective voice, it is in the hypocritical attitude that gave the bracero workmen's compensation under the clauses of Public Law 78 *while denying protection to U.S. citizens!* The Mexican national was paid $3000 for total permanent disability; his beneficiary received $2000 in the event of death. The American, exposed to one of the highest accident rates in industry, got nothing! Progressive legislators have repeatedly introduced bills that would remedy the inequity, but the few that have been passed are shamefully inadequate. The anachronism of agribusiness is apparent when it is considered that Maryland passed the first workmen's compensation law in 1902, a move followed by practically all other states before 1920.

II

The cynical outlook of many growers is reflected in
the comment of a large bean grower, as quoted by Father
George H. Dunne, S.J. The grower had fought efforts to
provide minimum schooling for the children of migrant
workers, children who, full-fledged field hands at nine
years of age, are doomed by illiteracy to a dreary life of
servitude. Said he: "When a migrant goes to school beyond the seventh grade, you've ruined a good bean
picker."

Father Dunne was outraged: "It may be objected that
the bean grower is not typical. The objection does not
stand up. He *is* typical of Americans who make their
money growing beans or tomatoes or lettuce or fruits.
The proof lies in the fact that the farm lobby bitterly
opposed this same effort, as it and the ranchers' association generally have coldly and successfully resisted for
years every effort to improve the wretched lot of the
migrant field hand. He is also typical of other average
Americans who are unmoved by, and indifferent to, the
miserable exploitation of the migrant worker.

". . . There are perhaps no people more generous with
their wealth than Americans, but the image which im-
pinges itself upon the world consciousness is not one of
American largesse. . . . It is not the exceptional Tom
Dooley, but the hard-nosed bean grower who appears to
be the normal product and expression of the social and
economic system which has reached its highest development in America. This, as much as anything else, is what

'colonialism' and 'imperialism' mean to downtrodden people everywhere. This is why there is so much anti-Americanism about."

The crying need for collective bargaining in the fields is plain; it remains to be seen where and how the movement will advance. Cannery and packinghouse workers have been organized for years, but there has not been a counterpart to the bracero to keep their movement fragmented. Certainly the furious battle of agribusiness to retain braceroism has not been based on any real indispensability of the bracero. *Even at the height of the program in California he was only one out of every six workers.* The bracero's true value has been as a pawn to checkmate the union movement. Once he passes forever from the scene, unionization is inevitable. To the majority of ranchers grown accustomed to unilateral advantage, the thought of labor-management dialogue is unthinkable. As one grower put it: "The handwriting may be on the wall, but we'll do everything possible to slow down unionization."

As the nucleus of the work force, the bracero has been an effective union-buster. The domestic reduced to the role of supplementary labor is deprived of a free marketplace in which to auction his services: if he refused to work at artificially depressed levels, growers happily marked him "unavailable" and brought in another bracero. The American trotted drearily along in a squirrel cage, bedeviled by the thought that in any other industry, a "labor shortage" would improve his chances of organizing and bettering his lot.

The hypocrisy of the bracero system was forcefully brought home to American workers in their intermittent attempts to gain recognition by striking. The spectacle of foreign "supplemental" workers being used as strike-breakers is without parallel in the annals of American labor. Several instances illustrate the point:

From 1947 to 1949 the National Farm Workers Union sought recognition from the Di Giorgio Fruit Corporation at Arvin, California. Government officials openly escorted braceros through the union's picket lines. Use of braceros was the decisive factor in breaking the strike.

In the fall of 1950 in the San Joaquin Valley, Highway patrolmen and private police escorted some 2000 braceros behind picket lines and broke a strike of 3500 tomato pickers.

In April, 1951, in California's Imperial Valley, workers organized by the National Farm Labor Union demanded the removal of wetbacks, the illegal border-hoppers who find ready employment at bargain basement wages. The wetbacks were removed, but were replaced by braceros escorted through the picket lines by armed guards.

In the spring of 1952 domestic cantaloupe workers in the Imperial Valley struck against wage slashes brought about by braceroism. The Department of Labor procrastinated through the remainder of the season in deciding whether a labor dispute under the rules did exist. During this time growers were authorized to bring in braceros to work under the slashed wage scale.

Between 1954 and 1959 the United Packinghouse Workers of America, AFL-CIO, conducted several strikes in protest over the relocation of packing-shed operations into the fields where braceros took over at about half the prevailing rate. These strikes were broken by the unrestricted use of braceros behind the union picket line.

In the winter of 1961 the newly formed Agricultural
Workers Organizing Committee, AFL-CIO, supported by
the Packinghouse Workers, attempted to organize workers
harvesting the winter lettuce crop in the lush govern-
ment-irrigated Imperial Valley. In the thirties, such efforts had often resulted in the organizers being beaten,
tarred, and feathered. The 3000 domestic workers were
vastly outnumbered by 7000 braceros. The domestics
wanted a pay raise from ninety cents to $1.25 an hour.
Even though the Mexican minister in Washington sought
the removal of braceros at the struck ranches, they stayed
—and broke the back of the strike.

This sad chronicle points up only too vividly that the
underdog American worker must buck not only powerful growers, but sometimes federal and state officials and
law-enforcement officers as well. As long as the bracero
loomed as a strikebreaker, the odds were long. Now at
last there is a ray of hope. In May, 1965, the Agricultural
Workers Organizing Committee (AWOC) struck Coa-
chella Valley, California, grape growers who were paying
sub-bracero wages of $1.25. The growers had not re-
quested braceros and therefore were not technically
under the Labor Department's criterion of $1.40. But
the strike, which idled about 1000 domestics, forced
growers to accede to the $1.40 mark. Although AWOC
failed to win recognition for itself, the strike marked the
first time growers had met in formal talks with union
leaders and agreed to demands. And it was the first time
in recent years that a substantial number of workers
dared join in a strike.

Again and again David, the farm worker, has pitted

his strength against that of Goliath, the powerful grower. Again and again David has been defeated.

But the second 1965 strike—the one that started on September 8—suggests that after years of suffering and disappointment the worker may yet succeed in having his basic human dignity acknowledged.

It was the Filipino farm workers in the Delano area of California's San Joaquin Valley who began the new strike, too. Weary of abuse and low wages they asked to be represented by the Agricultural Workers Organization Committee (AWOC) of the AFL-CIO. AWOC united nearly 1000 Filipino workers around Delano— the biggest table-grape producing area in the nation. Under the leadership of Larry Itliong, the Filipino workers decided to strike for not only better wages but union recognition as well. Within two days nearly the entire Filipino work force was out of the field. Growers immediately retaliated by shutting off labor-camp utilities, ordering foremen to toss workers' belongings from bunkhouses, and summoning sheriff's deputies to roust workers off the camp premises.

On September 16, 1965, more than 1500 members of the Farm Workers Association in Delano voted unanimously to join the strike. (The Farm Workers Association was established in Delano three years ago by Cesar Chavez. FWA provides over 2000 Mexican-American and Puerto Rican farm workers with services such as a credit union and a food and service station co-op.) A joint Strike Committee was established by the FWA's Chavez and AWOC's statewide director, Al Green.

The chief demand of both AWOC and FWA is for union recognition. The grape pickers asked for a wage increase to $1.40 per hour and twenty-five cents per box. A few growers were paying more but others were paying $1.20 per hour and ten cents a box at the time of the strike, and in recent years payment has been as low as nine cents per box and *no* hourly wage. The strikers also sought the enforcement of state laws providing for field toilets, sanitary drinking water, and rest periods—which are now widely violated.

To make their demands known the strikers sent registered letters to all thirty-seven growers in the four-hundred-square-mile strike area. Only three accepted the letter. Then telegrams were dispatched, but again only a few were accepted. Several growers have privately expressed their desire to negotiate, but they fear punitive action by their own private associations, especially the Agricultural Labor Bureau.

To undercut sympathy for the strike among workers who were undecided or fearful, growers hiked piece rates up and in many instances also raised hourly wages as soon as the strike was called. Nevertheless, by September 22 the work force in the strike area had been greatly reduced. On September 23, however, hastily recruited workers began to arrive from Bakersfield, Fresno, and Los Angeles. In violation of the California Labor Code, they had not been told of the strike by their recruiters. Most refused to enter the fields when they saw what was going on. The growers then brought labor from as far away as Texas. These workers, too, were not told of the strike, and when they arrived they were torn between sympathy for the strikers and their own need to earn at least enough money to return home. Despite their dilemma, many out-of-state workers left the fields and

joined other strikers attempting to find work outside the
strike area. In Bakersfield and other potential recruitment
centers growers sponsored radio broadcasts stating that
the strike was over, a bald falsehood. When the striking
unions placed legal pickets around their fields, growers
moved in heavy equipment and noisemaking devices to
prevent fieldworkers from seeing or hearing the pickets.

Growers then turned to more violent acts to discourage
strikers, with little hindrance from local law-enforcement
authorities. Striking workers have been run down or
threatened while local sheriff's deputies stood idly by.
On September 25, Jack Radovich, a member of a grower's
family, drove a poison-spray rig down a public road and
covered sixteen pickets with deadly sulphur spray. As he
passed the last picket he turned around and laid a
second cloud over half the group. Sheriff's deputies, who
had watched the entire episode from the beginning, finally
intervened. All of the pickets were temporarily blinded,
some so severely they did not recover for several days.
Strikers' complaints over such incidents have been either
ignored by local D.A.s or actually denied by on-the-scene
deputies.

There can not be the slightest question but that in
general the sympathies of the local police were with the
growers, not the workers. Growers succeeded in getting
a temporary court order against—what would you think?
Physical violence against strikebreakers? Destruction of
equipment? Sabotage of valuable vines? No, none of these
things was feared because the growers were well aware
that *the philosophy underlying the strike is nonviolence
and peaceful protest.* The court order was against "shout-

ing," apparently the worst charge that could be brought against the strikers.

A sympathetic minister, to test the validity of the order, started to read Jack London's definition of a strikebreaker to a group of scabs picking grapes. After a warning to lower his voice, he was carted off to jail. The charge: "disturbing the peace."

A few days later a group of forty-four workers, students, and ministers also shouted the world "*Huelga,*" Spanish for "strike," from a picket line. They too were arrested, for failure to disperse and for trespassing. Among those jailed were mothers, leaving over eighty children motherless for a few days.

I arrived in Delano about ten o'clock on a cool, overcast morning, met Cesar Chavez at Farm Workers Association headquarters, inspected the small, run-down "headquarters," where the strikers' paper *El Malcriado,* is published, and then went directly to a nearby field where a picket line had been set up. What I saw reminded me of a scene from the great Italian motion picture *The Organizer.* Poor strikers marching and shouting while, in the field, a short distance away, equally poor strikebreakers toiled away, keeping their eyes averted and pretending not to hear the arguments, entreaties, and denunciations that were called out to them. Some of those working appeared to be no more than fifteen years of age. I wondered why they were not in school. Probably only a city dude would ask such a question.

Talking to the strikers I could see that, although the struggle is costing them dearly, they are prepared for a long strike. They have heard that the sugar workers on Hawaii plantations took sixteen months to win. The mood of *la huelga* is one of hope and determination, partly because it is also a drive by Spanish-speaking Americans to join the civil rights movement begun by Negroes.

To Cesar Chavez, the heroic founder and director of the FWA, what is going on is much more than a demand for better pay and working conditions. The son of migrant parents, Chavez grew up in labor camps and farm towns in California. His organization is more a movement than a union. Now three years old, the 2000-member FWA has, beside its own credit union, an unheard-of achievement, an insurance program, the newspaper *El Malcriado*, and a grievance committee to investigate job misrepresentations and file compensation-insurance claims for members who cannot read or write English.

Chavez, Itliong, and their followers are well aware that the fundamental issue at stake is the right of collective bargaining. The workers ask nothing more important than the simple right to participate in discussions concerning their own living and working conditions. Their demands are not heedless. They so fully appreciate the growers' problems—perishable crops, unsteady markets—that they are willing to write a no-shutdown clause into their contracts. What they can no longer in good conscience tolerate is the papa-knows-best attitude whereby the growers decide and publicly announce what it is that their workers need and want.

If any men are entitled to speak for the workers it is Itliong and Chavez. Itliong, a short, graying Filipino who has lost his right hand, is a poor man whose sin in the eyes of growers is that he is standing up and demanding decent and dignified treatment for his fellows.

Chavez is also slight of stature, modest, soft-spoken,

poor, and courageous. He has been offered a $21,000-a-
year government job but prefers to stay with his people.
Mother Mary Xavier, O.S.U., of Novato, California, one
of his dear friends, says he is not only a highly intelligent
and gifted organizer, but also a "humble and deeply spiritual Christian with a cause that is just." Under his leadership, she says, the grape strike is "one of the most significant breakthroughs for social justice in California's long
history."

Nor is Mother Mary the only friend Cesar and his
strikers have within the church.

Almost daily there is renewed evidence of support from
the clergy. In November two priests who fly their own
airplane countered a technique that growers had devel-
oped of moving their workers to the center of picket fields
so that they could not hear the strikers. Father Keith
Kenny of Sacramento and Father Arnold Meagher of
Woodland, California—accompanied by Chavez—flew over
the fields and broadcast a loudspeaker appeal to strikebreakers to quit working and support the strike. Several
crews walked out of the fields after hearing the message.
Father Kenny of Our Lady of Guadalupe Church in Sacramento, later said, "The strike is a movement by the poor
people themselves to improve their condition. Where the
poor are, Christ should be, and is."

Because growers are importing outside strikebreakers,
the Catholic Bishop of El Paso, Bishop Sidney Metzger,
has urged workers in his area *not* to accept work in the
Delano fields. Father John Wagner, secretary of the
Catholic Bishops' Committee for the Spanish Speaking,
has also visited Delano, encouraged the strikers, and said
that they are setting a good example for the poor field

laborers of Texas. And Father James Vizzard, S.J., of the National Catholic Rural Life Conference, went to Delano, made a cash contribution to help the strikers, and told Cesar Chavez, one of the strike leaders, that if he could he would serve on the picket line himself.

Since almost all the striking vineyard workers are Catholic, it was not surprising they would receive support from priests and nuns. But what has been additionally encouraging is the help they've gotten from Protestant and Jewish groups as well. The Methodist Board of Social Concern, for example, recently passed a strong resolution favoring the organization of farm workers and asking its member churches to support the Delano strike with donations of food, clothing, and money. And the Western Association of Reform Rabbis, at its annual convention, not only voted full support for the workers but also commended the consumer boycott of Delano grapes and wine products.

Father Victor Salandini of Washington, D.C., has written to *El Malcriado:* "Thank you for your letter authorizing me to represent the National Farm Workers Association in any matters pertaining to legislative activities. I read Father Vizzard's wonderful letter . . . last week and I would like to say with Father Vizzard that if I could I'd be on the picket line myself with your workers. . . . *Viva La Causa!*"

As might have been expected there are those among the local Delano clergy, however, who know what side their bread is buttered on and therefore have either remained neutral in the controversy or else have sided with the growers. Their position is remarkably like that of those clergymen in the South who for two hundred years have been afraid to speak out for social justice for Negroes simply because such public statements would expose them to the disapproval, or worse, of the power elite. It is, after all, somewhat easier to be brave about Birmingham and Selma if one lives in Milwaukee. And it is easier to be brave about what is going on in Delano if one's church is not located in the immediate vicinity.

This category does not include, of course, that thankfully small percentage of the clergy who are as reactionary in this context as they have always been in others and who therefore could not be expected to give more than lip service, and precious little of that, to the cause of social justice for farm workers.

Says the Rev. Wayne C. Hartmire, Jr., director of the California Migrant Ministry: "The present situation poses a difficult dilemma for the churches. Charitable services, long the mainstay of Protestant penetration into poverty areas, are now problematic. The expectations of low-income people are revolutionary and not evolutionary. They want justice now and not special services for an unjust interim."

It is obvious that real alleviation of the pitiful conditions of farm labor means unionization. Appeals to Christian ethics fall on deaf ears; some growers are no more than pharisees to whom religion is not a living thing. The Rev. Hartmire, observing that "most churchmen in rural areas are misled into a safe, accommodating position by a steady stream of employer-orientated propaganda," paraphrased the reaction of the farm worker to church inertia: "You Christians speak brave words about Alabama but when the money changers are in your own temples then you stand for gradualism—gradualism which means justice can wait for those of us who don't pay our way in those temples." Growers, added the Rev. Hartmire, are a potent force in the church—"highly visible in a way that slum realtors, for example, are not."

The same scrupulous neutrality, which works to the advantage of the status quo, is sometimes seen in the posture of certain representatives of the Catholic hierarchy. Several years ago, for example, Father Thomas McCullough, a Spanish-speaking priest, was silenced by the Bishop of San Diego following grower complaints that he had participated in a field workers' rally in El Centro, in the Imperial Valley. In June, 1965, Father Salandini, then the pastor of a church in the border community of San Ysidro, was relieved of his duties by the San Diego prelate following his participation in organizing an AWOC chapter which struck five large tomato farms in the area. Father Salandini said he was "merely following papal social doctrine that a priest be concerned with the needs of the poor." Blaming the removal on "pressures by influential growers," the priest explained why he had become involved: "I grew up on a farm and worked in the fields as a boy and a young man for eleven years until I was ordained—and know how farm labor has been abused."

Neither Itliong nor Chavez is bitter about the opposition of a few clergymen. Chavez founded the Farm Workers Association partly on the inspiration of the late Pope John, who said: "We for that matter express our satisfaction with those sons of ours throughout the world who are actively engaged in the movement of agricultural workers with the intention of elevating the economic and social level of the communities of agricultural workers."

"And," adds Chavez, "the only real way to fight poverty here is with a union contract."

The nation-wide consumer boycott of Delano Grapes and Schenley Products in support of this end was launched in December 1965. Its first sponsor was an ad-hoc committee named The Los Angeles Friends of the Grape Strikers, consisting of members of religious groups, civil rights groups (SNCC and CORE), human rights organizations, political action groups, and concerned people from the labor movement.

Informational pickets were stationed at major supermarkets that stock Delano grapes and Schenley liquors and wines, although the boycott is not directed at markets or their employees.

Schenley was singled out not because it was paying especially low wages (because of the strike it had raised its pay scales considerably) but because it was the dominant power in the area with its 4500 acres of vineyards. The theory is that if Schenley could be induced to open discussions with Itliong and Chavez, the other growers would probably have to follow suit.

Schenley, in other parts of the country, has an admirable labor-relations record. It's executives in the East, for example, are civilized and progressive-minded citizens. But even they are wary of the strength of the California agribusiness forces. But a better distribution of agribusiness wealth is inevitable. The president of Schenley industries, according to *The Wall Street Journal* of January 26, 1966, has a personal income that ranges between one million and two million dollars per year. This fact must have *some* relevance to the plight of poor laborers trying to raise families on inadequate weekly salaries.

Despite growing sympathy for the strike, however, I do not foresee an early end to the controversy. The growers are wealthy and powerful, and they say that up to now the boycott has not hurt them. Some, in fact, claim they've just brought in the greatest harvest they've ever had.

In Delano I had an illuminating talk with one grower, Buddy Steele. Steele's argument is the same one that management has advanced for almost a century of labor-union controversy. He says that his workers are perfectly happy and don't want the union. He said that if they *did* want a union then he'd be over a barrel, and he and the other growers would have to concede the workers' freedom to organize in defense of their rights.

I'm willing to assume Steele's honesty and good will in making this statement, although I believe that his own self-interest has blinded him to the real wishes of the laborers, who work long hours at exhausting tasks for low pay. If I were an employer and were really certain that my workers didn't want a union I would call for an election immediately, to let the workers themselves democratically decide the issue. Unfortunately the growers are against such a democratic vote.

The situation clearly points to the need for bringing American farm labor under the protection of the National Labor Relations Act, something that Sen. Harrison Williams, chairman of the Senate Subcommittee on Migratory Labor, has advocated for years. Presidential commissions have urged the same course, but so far powerful agribusiness interests have discouraged such legislation.

What are the counter arguments of the growers? They are few and simple. Some say: "Unions? Never!" Others say: "Unions only if our workers need and want them. But they don't."

The arguments of some growers are best refuted by the words and actions of other growers. Consider:

1. Growers say that Delano boasts the best farm wages in California and that the workers are quite content with their pay rates, hours, and working conditions.

Growers tell of having, for many years, provided Christmas baskets for the needy workers.

Question: Do well-paid, contented workers and their families need Christmas baskets?

2. Ranchers argue that the controversy would dissolve if "outsiders" would stay out of the area. (Shades of Selma and Birmingham!)

On the other hand, growers' associations have spent large sums importing *outside* strikebreakers from points as distant as Texas and Mexico.

Not all workers in the Delano-Visalia-Earlimart area are on strike, of course. Growers suggest that the reason is that the workers are so content with their lot they have no interest in being organized. Such an argument is grossly misleading. Laborers still in the field fall into various catergories:

1. Those who are uninformed about the details of the struggle.

2. Those who are in sympathy with the strike but cannot afford to support families without their already meager income. Remember that big-city strikers can be sustained by full union treasuries; the coffers of the striking farm workers' groups are almost empty.

3. Those who are fearful of getting mixed up in an emotion-laden controversy in which the threat of physical violence is very real.

4. Those who are on friendly terms with a particular grower, contractor, or foreman and feel a personal loyalty that inhibits strike participation. One worker explained, "My foreman has loaned me money. I'd like to walk out but he's asked me to stay on and I feel I owe him something."

5. Those from other areas who were not told of the strike when recruited. Some in this category join the strikers, others drift away early, still others must work for a time to make going-home money. There are some lone wolves who, impressed by the high wages growers are now offering as extra inducement, see a chance to make a killing.

6. Those Mexican-Americans who see a chance to move up into the relative security of middle-class existence, by means of an acquaintance here, a relative there, or an opportunity for advancement. Such people, some of them Mexican Uncle Toms, are reluctant to get their hands dirty in a strike, afraid to risk their opportunity for social acceptance by antagonizing the local power elite.

It is easy for the detached observer to criticize such strikebreakers, but let the reader who has not been guilty of similar weakness cast the first stone at them. What is tragic is that they cannot see that the growers are interested, understandably enough, in the welfare of the growers and that so long as workers fail to cooperate they will be powerless, whereas in unity their strength could win the strike and introduce a glorious new day for California farm labor.

Such people, of course, have always played roles in the workingman's struggle for social justice. Eventually, after the battle is won by dedicated organizers and strikers, those who sat on the sidelines fall into line and reap the same benefits as those who sacrificed. Perhaps it is unjust but it is the way the world turns.

As this is written, the Delano strike is more than ten months old. The strikers are pitted against a formidable array of power, and a dramatic breakthrough is not imminent. Unfortunately Big Labor not only has failed to lend assistance to a significant degree, but frequently does not honor the farm workers' picket lines. This has been a two-edged sword slashing the workers' chances. Teamsters, for example, cross the picket lines to haul the grapes to market so that to some growers the strike is little more than the faint annoyance of a fly on the arm. And workers in the field are reluctant to go over to the other side of the picket lines because there is no substantial strike fund to sustain them when they get there.

The strike, therefore, could collapse at any time under the steady pressure of the growers' side. But if it does it will inevitably start up again soon. For there is now a close-knit comradery among the strikers that has been lacking before. Theirs is a movement with the structure of a union, but the spirit of a freedom struggle. On the picket lines during the day the cry is *"Huelga! Huelga!"* ("Strike! Strike!") After a communal supper in the evening the song is *"Nosotros Venceremos"* ("We Shall Overcome").

Theirs is a righteous cause, and this is its abiding strength.

P.S. As this manuscript goes to press Schenley Industries has just signed an agreement with the National Farm Workers Association and the Christian Brothers Wineries has also agreed to negotiate with Cesar Chavez's group. But the strike is not over. The majority of Delano growers still refuse to budge. The strikers are greatly encouraged but they know that the breakthrough, to paraphrase President Kennedy's observation about the nuclear test-ban treaty, is only the first small step on the thousand-mile journey toward social justice for the farm workers of the United States.

I2 CONCLUSION

I

I hope it will occur to the reader to wonder why I have bothered to write a book about a social problem concerning which I could not be considered an authority. The answer is that if any appreciable number of average citizens were studying the already available literature, all would be well. Unfortunately this is not the case. Since as a public figure I have some ready call upon the public ear, I decided to prepare this book as both a statement of my personal concern—which I hope the reader has been induced to share—and a report of the stark realities of an ugly chapter in modern American history.

For over thirty years all sorts of documentaries, reports, studies, and books have been disseminated concerning the plight of migratory and other farm workers and their

CONCLUSION 129

families. Religious organizations, citizens' groups, trade unions, Congressional committees, and government agencies have studied the problem and made numerous specific recommendations for reform. And yet until the present time little enough has been accomplished as a result.

In the Depression, John Steinbeck aroused the national conscience with his unforgettable book *The Grapes of Wrath*. It moved a committee of the Senate to attempt—with scant success—to correct some of the inequities of our farm labor system. Additional Congressional investigations came in the forties and fifties, but for the most part little or nothing was done to correct the abuses such committees pointed to. In 1951, President Truman's Commission on Migratory Labor prepared what was surely the most comprehensive report of the problem ever published, complete with detailed recommendations covering every conceivable phase of the migratory labor dilemma. But year after year went by with the great majority of the Truman Commission recommendations still not acted upon, largely because the needed reforms were bitterly resisted by powerful growers' associations.

One of the depressing things about the farm labor controversy is that it has such a musty, mid-thirties air about it. One would have thought that the nation had substantially settled the arguments that divided labor and management during the years of the Depression. Indeed most Americans today do assume that such issues were long ago settled once and for all. But—as I have explained —they were not settled so far as farm laborers are concerned. Farm employer attitudes are, therefore, some thirty years behind the times. When the Agricultural Workers' Organizing Committee employed the device of

the strike in the Imperial Valley in an attempt to up-
grade working conditions there, the growers used every
classic method of union-busting related in the history of
the American labor movement. Armed guards and police-
men became a common sight, strikeleaders and individual strikers were intimidated, beaten, jailed, or run
out of town.

II

Year after year there is a sameness, even—so soon does
the human conscience develop an insensitivity to what
should always be heart-rending details—a monotony to
the reports. Consider, for example, the following three
examples from various sources in 1961, all of which could
have been heard in 1931, 1941, or 1951: "Here in the
heart of the nation's richest farm country (California's
central valley) four hundred members of farm labor families are sweating out the harvest in eighteenth-century
conditions. Most of the one-room shacks have eight to
ten occupants. One spigot supplies water for the entire
camp." (The New York *Times,* July 30, 1961.)

"I came away angry and sick from the tomato fields
just thirty miles south of the glitter and wealth of Miami
Beach. I found the same crude exploitation, the same
dreadful living conditions, just thirty miles south of New
York City." (Dale Wright. "The Forgotten People," Series
in the New York *World-Telegram and Sun,* October 23,
1961.)

"John Morrison, thirty-eight-year-old migrant laborer
from Southeastern Missouri, dropped his hoe after ten

hours of chopping cotton on the J. E. Pollard farm here (in eastern Arkansas) yesterday and collected three dollars for another day's work . . . his wife and their flushed eleven-year-old daughter, who had weeded cotton under the hot sun all day alongside them, piled into their 1946 Buick along with the Morrison's eight-month-old baby and nine-'year-old daughter (and headed for Michigan) . . . 'to see if we can find work in the cherry orchards.'" (The New York *Times*, July 16, 1961.)

One of the many unfortunate effects of living conditions such as those described is that the segregation of the poor tends to make them seem like creatures of a different breed. Truman Moore, in *The Slaves We Rent*, relates the story told him by a migrant minister in Florida who received a call from a woman who said her club wanted to bring a Christmas dinner out to the migrant labor camp. He told her it was a fine idea. "Now tell me," the woman said, "what do they like to eat?"

We have no right to insulate ourselves against the unpleasant realities by thinking of the poor in statistical terms, or supposing that they are generally much like ourselves except that they do not have much money. To be poor in this world is by no means merely a matter of having less money than one's neighbor. I stress again that it is also to be without decent clothing, without enough food or the proper kind of food, to be without decent shelter, and frequently to exist in a blind alley of despair where one sees no hope of finding a way out. To be poor is also to lack the respect of others and finally to have one's respect for one's self weakened.

The president of a multimillion grower-packer-shipper citrus farm told Moore, "Migrants are the scum of the earth. Anything they get over forty cents an hour is gravy."

I am reminded of the Dr. Poole, who, in arguing with Florence Nightingale that the British soldier was not worth her tender concern, referred to him as "the scum of the earth." The great woman reminded him that such "scum" had down through the centuries steadfastly defended the British Empire and had frequently exhibited the most glorious heroism, something scarcely to be expected of scum. So too, the modern conservative farm operators who refer to the farm labor force as "the scum of the earth" overlook that without such workers America would not eat and that in any event a worker is still a human being, an American citizen and a child of God, and is therefore entitled to all the respect logically implied in our assertion that America's chief superiority over the Communist world lies in our insistence on the dignity of the individual.

Wealthy growers sometimes echo the ancient management argument to the effect that the poor laboring man is somehow not entitled to comforts and niceties because "if you give 'em bathtubs, they'll just use 'em to store coal in." Such blanket accusations cannot possibly be true of all members of a societal group, however underprivileged and degraded. But a more important fact is that even if the growers were correct in their condemnation of the workers it should still be recognized that such social degradation—since it was *not* something the individual worker was born with—must therefore be an *effect* caused by his environment. The solution, obviously, is to change the environment so that it no longer produces people without enough sense to use bathtubs for their rightful purpose.

III

It was once possible for men to argue whether or not specific social changes—or social change in general—ought to occur or could be prevented from occurring, but it is now clear that change is inevitable. This does not mean that advocates of any specific alteration in the structure of a society are entitled to argue that *it* is inevitable; obviously this is not the case as regards various individual propositions. But it does suggest that the process of social evolution has not suddenly frozen stock-still for what would certainly be the first time in all human history. We ought not, therefore, pointlessly discharge our energies trying to reverse this historic and inevitable process, but rather should seek to guide its course. And the need to do so was never more urgent, for not only is change still occurring, but it is happening now at an increasingly accelerated pace, thus adding a special dimension to problems already urgent and precarious enough.

Am I talking about equality? Not really, not here. I agree with the conservative view that equality sought merely for its own sake is meaningless. Since no two things in the universe are identical, it therefore follows that no two men are precisely equal, and since there is no equality in nature, it would seem reasonable to assume that equality as an ideal is without substance. This view, however, can never be put forth as justification of the gross injustices and inequalities that to this day abound in every corner of the earth. The human verdict has long since been given about those individuals who accumulate enormous concentrations of wealth and power not necessarily because they are superior in intelligence or virtue but sometimes because—by accident of birth, commercial timing, or some quality of aggressive selfishness—they have stored up in their vaults treasures that, if equitably distributed, could support the families of 10,000 honest workingmen.

The argument continues in which conservatives argue that not the state but private, voluntary charitable effort should solve the problems of poverty. But if we shift our attention from abstractions to reality we observe that while the conservatives *talk* about this approach it is almost invariably the progressive, openhearted sort of person who actually does the necessary works of mercy. Where, for example, are the Young Americans For Freedom in the Peace Corps, Operation Head Start, the Mental Health campaign, Synanon, VISTA, the civil rights movement, and so forth?

Conservatives pose as allies of the Judeo-Christian tradition, as friends of the church—often sincerely—until there is a conflict between their economic practices and their religious principles. Then two things usually occur: (1) they resolve the impasse in favor of their pocketbooks, not their prayerbooks, and (2) they produce materialist rationalizations according to their economic philosophy and make little further reference to *spiritual* standards.

The new status-quo camp includes a handful of honest intellectuals who concern themselves with issues of political morality, but these scholars are being used—by cer-

tain individuals with cold cynicism—to provide a rationalization that masks a reversion to economic practices upon
which the American people turned their backs over a
quarter of a century ago.

In the thirties—after debate lasting almost a century—
the people, rising up in that magnificent and socially
effective indignation that is one of the glorious fruits of
the tree of republican democracy, put a stop to the
immoral and un-American exploitation of laboring men,
women, and children that had been so common. The
people, in other words, voted themselves a larger measure
of that social justice to which their spiritual tradition,
their political philosophy, and their common sense told
them they were entitled. The creation of such welfare-
state benefits as unemployment compensation, Social Security, factory-safety laws, the passage of the Wagner
Act, child-labor laws—these and other boons to the
workingman—was widely hailed as signaling a new dawn
of economic security and freedom.

This process was not made literally over the dead bodies
of those entrenched exploiters who had all their lives
exhibited such scant regard for the dignity of those children of God entrusted to their care. It is better to say that
such progress was made not over their dead bodies but
over their dead souls, for they did not retire gracefully
from the field of battle, but rather retreated and continued from that day to this as much sniping and even open
warfare against the ranks of labor as they thought they
could get away with.

Some of them—it is clear—have been getting away with
quite a bit.

IV

Is there then no hope at all for the poor farm worker? Quite the contrary. As Michael Harrington has written, "It is one of the terrible ironies of political life in America that there are social problems that could be dealt with, where the basic research has been done and the techniques of solution demonstrated, but where there is no political force strong enough to enforce progress. This is the case with farm poverty. It is, for example, completely obvious that these areas require comprehensive inventories, careful planning, and coordinated programs. The battle for this concept, lost in the debate over the depressed area's law, will be one of the most crucial conflicts in the sixties."

I do not want to give the impression that the face of the Southwestern elite is turned coldly toward the poor, period. Many dedicated individuals are deeply concerned about the problem. The war on poverty, of course, is not a new war. For years there have been individuals and organizations working to help the poor: good-will industries, the Salvation Army, Catholic, Protestant, and Jewish charitable groups, legal-aid societies—these and others have long been active in helping the unfortunate. Such forces might be considered lonely advance scouts, many of whom have struggled for years against what have always been in one sense hopeless odds. Sometimes their activity was aggressive guerrilla warfare, other times it was a holding action, and frequently they have suffered outright defeat. But they have been active nevertheless in

the war on poverty. Imagine the sense of encouragement
and cheer they now feel at knowing that the rest of the
nation is—at long last—being enlisted in that war.

V

The Emergency Committee to Aid Farm Workers is
a civic organization with offices in Los Angeles. It was
established by a group of concerned citizens for the purpose of providing farm labor families with direct personal
encouragement and assistance in their efforts to remedy
the distressing living conditions under which many of
them live. Its guiding principle is that one of the responsibilities of the agricultural industry in the United
States—along with all other business—is to assure a decent
American standard of living for its workers.

A visit to the rough, simple Emergency Committee
headquarters in an old shop in Oxnard is an inspiring
experience. You immediately feel the great sense of sympathetic concern for the workers that motivates the members of the committee staff and you are seized, too, by
the hopeful and optimistic outlook for the future, although
no informed person supposes that progress is going to be
easy and all downhill.

The committee members are eager to tell you, for example, of Operation Buenaventura, a plan approved
under the War on Poverty Program. It is a $106,000 pilot
project designed to educate and train twelve farm workers
as community leaders and worker-advisors. Its director
is Mrs. Katherine Peake, a dedicated middle-aged woman
who has long fought the good fight for the benefit of the

friendless farm workers about whom she cares so deeply.

Operation Buenaventura is the only project of its kind in the nation, Mrs. Peake explains. "We call it an inoculation against poverty." Federal endorsement requires that at least ten per cent of the funds for the program come from the local community in the form of donations, materials, or volunteer labor. And residents of Oxnard's "colonia," the farm worker's quarter, are determined to make good their contribution. When I visited the area they were already at work landscaping the dusty, weed-grown corner lot at 506 Cooper Road, cleaning and re-painting a pair of dilapidated and ancient buildings to get them ready for the first group of students, who began their training on July 15.

By mid-June a citizens' committee of Ventura County residents had already begun to screen applicants. Committee members included John Flynn, a Ventura high school teacher, Captain A. Walker of the Salvation Army, Edwin Lang of the local district attorney's office, Rev. H. W. Washington of Oxnard's Trinity Baptist Church, and Ronald Benner, Executive Secretary of the County Building's Trade Council. Farm worker members of the committee were Richard Ayala, George Morales, Marcos Rayna, Theresa Urquidez, and Connie Kozakowski.

The objective of the program is to develop indigenous leadership among the workers themselves, leadership that can be effective in reaching the larger community of farm laborers and involving more of them in the personal working-out of solutions for their many problems. The trainees are receiving ten months of instruction and practical experience in methods of dealing with the life-and-death issues that concern them. They are being taught, for example, how to deal with the various public and private agencies that are presumably concerned with their welfare, procedures for the successful processing of complaints against such agencies, a basic knowledge of the laws affecting them, and formulation and management of organizations for the benefit of the farm worker community, how to evaluate and take advantage of job opportunities, how to conduct meetings and discussion groups and how to conduct employer-employee transactions.

VI

I have seen poverty in other parts of the world, in France, in Italy, and the even more shocking conditions in Hong Kong and India. Conservative polemicists sometimes argue that although there are admittedly millions of Americans who are very poor, such people are still better off than the European, the Oriental, or the Latin-American poor. God, I would think that a man would blush to voice such arguments. If a neighbor has lost one leg, get him a crutch and help him to his feet, don't simply tell him that you know someone else who has lost *two* legs and then go on your way.

Though living conditions are indeed squalid for hundreds of thousands of Chinese residents of Hong Kong, the British and the city generally are at least bending every effort to alleviate the plight of such unfortunates. When I visited the city I saw that dozens of high-rise, low-rent apartment buildings had been constructed to take care of both the expanding local population and the swarms of immigrants who have come to the city from the Chinese mainland. If the beleaguered city of Hong Kong can make such efforts, then you are going to have to talk to me for a long time to convince me that similar efforts—appropriate, naturally, to specific local situations —cannot be made in this, the richest nation in all human history.

Somewhere a well-to-do farm owner is self-righteously criticizing Communist rulers for their refusal to let their subjects live with a proper measure of human dignity. But it may never occur to him that he is guilty of the same crime.

The enemies of our way of life around the world—as well as the uncommitted third of mankind—watch with great interest the way in which the United States is preparing to deal with the problem of poverty. Our critics say that we cannot solve the problem, that only a Marxist approach is equal to the task. Those of us who are convinced that such issues can be dealt with within the framework of the free-enterprise system had better get busy and do the job. The world will not wait forever to solve its dilemmas of poverty, ignorance, disease, hunger, and population pressure. Our example now is of literally historic importance.

We ought, in one sense, to be grateful for the challenges we face, for without challenge man does not grow. If you are never threatened you will never discover the degree of your courage. If you are never tempted you will not discover the degree of your virtue. If you are not puzzled you will not discover the degree of your intelligence. So now—though we are threatened, tempted, puzzled—we must not be discouraged, must not resort to the irrational search for a scapegoat, a Jonah—must not weaken, must not give way to hysteria, suspicion, fear, and hatred.

Rather we should search within ourselves for those resources which are given to all men, albeit in varying amounts. I refer to such resources as courage, integrity, sanity, charity, faith, and hope.

It would be easy to indulge in empty chauvinism and appeal to the reader's pride by referring to these as specifically American virtues. But we know that, while they have indeed helped make America great, God has not denied them to other cultures and societies. No, these are the fundamental *human* virtues. The reason for their existence is rooted in the essential mystery of the heart of man. They now can lead us toward social justice for those so poor that the ground is their table.